Literacy, Home and School

Literacy, Home and School:
Research and Practice in Teaching Literacy with Parents

Peter Hannon

 The Falmer Press

(A member of the Taylor & Francis Group)
London • Washington, DC

UK   The Falmer Press, 4 John Street, London WC1N 2ET
USA   The Falmer Press, Taylor & Francis Inc., 1900 Frost Road, Suite 101, Bristol, PA 19007

First published in 1995

A catalogue record for this book is available from the British Library

Library of Congress Cataloging-in-Publication Data are available on request

ISBN 0 7507 0359 8 cased
ISBN 0 7507 0360 1 paper

Jacket design by Caroline Archer

Typeset in 10/12 pt Garamond by
Graphicraft Typesetters Ltd., Hong Kong.

Printed in Great Britain by Burgess Science Press, Basingstoke on paper which has a specified pH value on final paper manufacture of not less than 7.5 and is therefore 'acid free'.

Contents

List of Tables and Figures

Preface

In this book I address two concerns of educational systems throughout the world. One is what can be done to extend literacy and raise literacy standards for all sections of the population — a concern even in countries where the majority has been literate for several generations. Another is the relation between home learning and school learning and what should be the role of parents in children's education — something now being rethought in many long-established school systems. The book focuses on the intersection between these two: how to improve the teaching of literacy through involving parents.

I deal with three issues in particular. First, because I have been dissatisfied with the atheoretical, ahistorical and apolitical character of much discussion about parental involvement in the teaching of literacy, I wanted to explore some issues underlying the nature of literacy, recent changes in home–school relations, and the rationale for parental involvement (Chapters 1, 2 and 3). I believe that practice in this field would be improved if it was more firmly grounded in theory. Second, I wanted to write about a number of studies that I have carried out with colleagues in Sheffield over the years. These have been reported in publications scattered in various journals and books but not always easily accessible to general readers. I wanted to assemble the pieces into one picture. The Sheffield studies chiefly concern work with parents in the pre-school years (Chapter 4) and aspects of involvement in the teaching of reading in the early school years (Chapters 5 and 6). I also discuss some other forms of involvement (Chapter 7) but in less detail. Third, as I am committed to research as one means of renewing and developing practice, I wanted to argue for certain ways of doing and using research in this field (Chapters 8, 9, 10 and 11). I suggest methods of evaluation, and try to assess what we have learned and what we still need to know.

Since moving, several years ago, from teaching in a school to teaching and researching in a university, I have had the privilege of working with many teachers carrying out studies of various aspects of parental involvement and literacy. They have invariably demonstrated that teachers carrying out their own research — and building on that of others — illuminates day to day practice and enables it to develop in new directions. Several will find their work referred to in this book alongside that of non-teacher researchers.

I have tried to speak directly to teachers, particularly those who share my excitement about developments in this field and who have some curiosity about what a research perspective currently offers. I hope that others, including headteachers, home–school liaison teachers, advisers, teacher trainers, policy makers, and some parents, will find something of value in it. As I also want the book to be part of my dialogue with fellow researchers in the field, I hope that they too will find ideas here worth debating or extending. The danger, of course, is that in trying to engage with readers having such diverse interests and backgrounds, I will eventually frustrate or disappoint all of them. I trust that readers' skills are such that they know how to skip what does not interest them, and to take whatever does in the order that suits them.

So much of what I have learned about literacy and parents has been learned from so many other people over the last decade or so that I do not know how to acknowledge their contributions fully. I am very conscious of all the teachers — many studying at Sheffield University — who have generously shared their experience, ideas and discoveries with me. Other teachers — and parents — have cooperated in numerous research studies. However, certain colleagues and collaborators have been particularly influential in extending my thinking. The first was Jack Tizard. He and Jenny Hewison first made me aware of the significance of parental involvement in the teaching of reading. I have since been fortunate, in a series of research studies, in the colleagues with whom I have worked, including Angela Jackson, Beryl Page, Jo Weinberger, and Cathy Nutbrown. I owe a great deal to supportive colleagues in the Division of Education at Sheffield University. In the writing of this book Elaine Millard, Stephen Rowland and Jo Weinberger provided helpful criticisms of draft extracts.

My research over the years has benefited from support from the University of Sheffield Research Fund, the Department of Education and Science, the European Commission, a Kellmer Pringle Fellowship, and an ESRC Personal Research Grant.

I owe most to my family. I much appreciate their tolerance and support, especially over Easter 1994 when I did little else but write. Because of the particular topic of the book, I have a further debt. My two children, Laura and Celia, challenged and shaped my ideas about literacy development while also being intrinsic to my experience of the parent's role (they helped me to finish the book, too, by demanding their turn on the computer) and my wife, Valerie, has shown in countless ways how a parent enables children's literacy to develop.

Peter Hannon
Sheffield
June, 1994

Chapter 1

The Meaning of Literacy

Imparting literacy to the next generation has historically been seen as the task of schools. However, in this book I argue that much of children's literacy learning takes place before school or out of school — mainly in fact, at home. This is a challenge for schools. Instead of relying on in-school learning to promote literacy, the problem is how to build upon or extend at-home learning. The key is to involve parents more in the teaching of literacy — a part of their children's education from which they have often been excluded. I hope to show how teachers can work with parents, not only in the school years, but also before children start school, how involvement can be achieved in various ways, and how these deserve further development and evaluation.

Before getting into the detail of what should be done, this first chapter seeks to justify some assumptions. These are: that literacy is important for children and adults; that it is unequally distributed in society and strongly related to home experiences; that literacy teaching should always be part of some wider concern; and that we have to be careful about which kinds of literacy we promote. This will help identify some implications for how we can begin to think about school–home relationships in this field.

Is Literacy Really that Important?

Today, there is widespread anxiety about literacy in almost all countries throughout the world. In those where large sections of the population are illiterate, universal literacy is seen as essential for reaching political, economic and health goals. But even in industrialized countries where there has been compulsory schooling for generations, there is concern about the persistence of a minority of illiterate adults, complaints about the inadequacy of workforce literacy skills needed for competition in international markets, and controversy about how children should be taught literacy.

Some of the literacy panic is probably attributable to the needs of politicians to generate anxiety about matters they can then make a show of tackling. It may be in the interests of some groups in society if the 'literacy crisis' diverts attention from other problems of social order, unemployment, or educational provision (or if it can be presented as the root cause of such problems). But does that mean that altogether too much is made of literacy and that there is no literacy problem? Does it matter whether all children are enabled to become fully literate? Does it matter whether children acquire their literacy in or out of school? To address these questions, I want to begin by re-examining the value of literacy — culturally, personally and educationally.

The Cultural Importance of Literacy

Literacy is the ability to use written language to derive and convey meaning. In the teaching of literacy one generation equips the next with a powerful cultural tool. Written language enables members of a culture to communicate without meeting; to express and explore their experience; to store information, ideas and knowledge; to extend their memory and thinking; and, increasingly nowadays, to control computer-based processes.

Communication between people who do not meet — and perhaps never could meet — is one of the most obvious uses for written language. This means, for example, at a mundane level, that parents can send a note to school to explain a child's absence or, at a more profound level, that a single author's work can reach millions of readers. The writers and readers who are in communication may know each other or they may be complete strangers, widely separated by distance and time. They may even be separated by many generations. The written language may be used for a letter, a financial transaction, a vehicle repair manual, a public record, a news report, a legal statute, a novel, a recipe, or a philosophical argument. Literacy means being able to make fuller use of such shared cultural resources and being able to interact more fully with an enormous range of other people.

Thus literacy means much more than just decoding letter–sound correspondences in reading or forming letters and spelling correctly in writing (vital though these skills are). No one reads simply to decode or writes simply to form letters. It is fundamentally a matter of understanding others' meanings or communicating meaningfully with them rather than exercising specific perceptual and motor skills.

In human history the development of written language must have meant a change of the same order as the earlier evolution of spoken language. Not only did writing facilitate within-group communication and recording for our ancestors but it greatly accelerated the process whereby one generation could build upon the accumulated knowledge of previous generations.

A key use of written language, from earliest times, has been to express and to explore human experience. At first this was in written versions of spoken forms such as stories, myths, songs, poetry or drama — written probably to aid memory. Subsequently, writing became more important in the development of these forms so that the written versions preceded the spoken ones. In many narrative genres (most obviously the novel) the written form stands alone. Children and adults who are able to read such material therefore have access to a vast and intricately depicted range of human experience and reflection stored in the literature of the world. For those who are illiterate in this sense, that door is closed.

Writers can also use written language to communicate with themselves. They may do so simply as an aid to memory when, for example, writing a shopping list or noting appointments in a diary. They are in effect writing to themselves in the future. It can go further, however, when an author seeks to organize his or her thoughts by writing them out, reading them (almost as if they were someone else's), reviewing, and then revising them. Howard Becker explains how such writing can aid thinking.

> First one thing, then another, comes into your head. By the time you have the fourth thought, the first one is gone. For all you know, the fifth thought is the same as the first . . . You need to give the thoughts a physical embodiment, *to put them down on paper.* A thought written down (and not immediately thrown into the wastebasket) is stubborn, doesn't change its shape, can be compared with the other thoughts that come after it. (Becker, 1986, pp.55–6)

The nature of literacy in a culture is repeatedly redefined as the result of technological changes. The introduction of new materials (stone tablets, skins, papyrus, paper) and new mark making methods (scratching, chiselling, ink, the printing press, typewriters, ballpoints, laser printers, and so on) has meant both new users and new uses for written language. The consequences of such changes can be very complex — not just in terms of *more* literacy but *different* literacy (Eisenstein, 1985). Our literacy today is consequently very different from that of medieval England not just because the printing press is more efficient than having scribes copy manuscripts in monasteries but also because printing and other technologies have stimulated entirely new uses for written language (e.g. tax forms, novels, postcards, advertisements) unimagined by medieval society.

Information technology today will have repercussions in the future that are hard to predict. Written language has taken on a new importance as a method of human–machine communication — usually in inputting instructions or data through a computer keyboard (i.e. writing) and in reading from a screen. This may eventually be superseded by other methods based on graphic displays and direct voice input/output but for reasons of speed and efficiency these will almost certainly still require literacy at least in being able to read messages on screen. It is sometimes claimed that advances in information technology reduce the need for literacy but this is to ignore the fact that a great deal of this technology is devoted to the storage, organization, and processing of *text*. On-line help systems are often heavily text dependent. Also, information technology appears to generate a huge amount of ancillary printed material in the form of user manuals, specialist magazines and other documentation. The idea that information technology might eliminate the need for children to acquire literacy is implausible — although it may well transform the nature of their literacy.

The Personal Value of Literacy

Imagine becoming, for some reason, unable to read or write but still having to live in a literate culture. What would it mean? For most readers of this book it would mean giving up their present employment, a massive loss of independence, and reliance on family, friends and others to accomplish the simplest tasks of everyday life. It would mean being denied all the uses of literacy discussed so far. The far reaching implications of such a personal disaster are a further measure of the value of literacy.

It is not just readers drawn from a narrow, highly educated section of society who value literacy. Anyone in an industrialized society who has difficulties in reading or writing immediately faces many other problems. There is the fear of being stigmatized as illiterate, which means that many go to extraordinary lengths to disguise their inability to use written language ('I haven't got my glasses' or 'I haven't got a pencil'). One could argue that this is simple prejudice — to be resisted like other kinds based on race, gender or disability — but illiteracy by itself and without any other social process means exclusion from many aspects of the culture whether it be reading books, football results, TV listings, food packaging or filling in simple forms and sending greeting cards. Job opportunities (and even the confidence to seek employment) are extremely limited or in some circumstances non-existent. The capacity to act as parents in modern society (or at least the ease with which it can be done) is severely limited. It is perfectly true that none of these problems would arise if society was less dependent on written language — in that sense one could 'blame' society rather than the individual — but that is little comfort for those concerned.

The meaning of literacy for those who have not acquired it is best expressed in their own words. This is what some young adults told interviewers in a national survey (ALBSU, 1987).

> I'm frightened if someone comes to the door with anything that has to be read. I couldn't fill in an application form for a job if I wanted to.

> I try to read books but I don't get any difficult words from them. If letters come someone has to read them for me.

> On a motorway I can't read the signs. At work I have problems with filling in the shipping sheets and things.

> It stops me getting a better job, a more secure one.

For adults who are parents, the difficulties can be particularly distressing.

My children are starting to read and I can't read stories to them.

It's embarassing — very embarassing in so many ways. For instance, if I send the kid to a shop I can't write out what I need.

I'd like to help my daughter with her school work. I can just cope at the moment but I won't be able to soon.

The stories of those without literacy tell us what it means for those who do have it. Case studies reported by Peter Johnston (1985) show how much people have to do to compensate for a lack of literacy. At school their coping strategies may include memorizing text, listening carefully for oral instructions, bluffing, relying on help from classmates. After leaving school the strategies identified by Johnston were mainly preventative — avoidance of print in any potentially social situation.

For example, Bill participates in business meetings for which and at which he must read material. His strategy is to be sure to spend some time 'shooting the breeze' with other participants before the meeting to pick up the gist of things. At the meeting he says nothing until asked for his opinion, by which time he has been able to gain enough information to respond. He reported that this also makes him appear conservative and thoughtful. Charlie reads the prices on gas pumps to get the right gas in his car and truck. He cannot read the words but uses the price hierarchy as his information source. Unlike many readers for whom the price is not so relevant, he always remembers the current prices. (Johnston, 1985, p.159)

Impressive as these strategies are, they do lead to problems. Bill was sometimes found out (trying to read to his young children, reading a paper at work); Charlie sometimes put diesel in his truck by mistake. Both were prone to severe and incapacitating anxiety when an encounter with written language could not be avoided.

Literacy in Education and Intellectual Development

Educationally, literacy is the key to the rest of the curriculum. Virtually all schooling, after the first year or two, assumes pupil literacy. This is particularly so to the extent that children are expected to work independently of teachers, for that requires them to read worksheets, written directions, reference materials, and so on. Many schools are anxious to encourage this pattern of pupil learning from the earliest possible stage — which means establishing literacy as soon as possible after school entry. The corollary is that children who find reading and writing difficult are disadvantaged in *all* areas of the curriculum.

The effectiveness of schools in establishing literacy has been a recurrent issue of controversy. In 1972 in England, for example, it led the government to set up the Bullock Committee to enquire into standards and methods of teaching. The Committee received evidence from many people who believed standards of literacy had fallen but it pointed out that similar complaints could be found in the Newbolt Report of 1921 where one employer had stated that 'teaching of English in present day schools produces a very limited command of the English language' (DES, 1975 p.3). The Bullock Report, although widely acclaimed by professionals in education and highly influential, did not silence critics for long. By the end of the 1980s the controversy had surfaced again and further reports were required (DES, 1990; Cato and Whetton, 1991). Parallel developments can be found in other industrialized countries.

Debates in this area are usually characterized by (or fuelled by) inadequate information about true levels of literacy — whether rising or falling — and deeply held convictions that one method or another is the only way to teach reading or writing. However, what they clearly demonstrate is how widely the teaching of literacy is considered an important matter — culturally and politically as well as educationally.

It has been argued by some educationists that literacy has profound consequences for intellectual development. Vygotsky suggested that writing means acquiring an explicit knowledge of the sounds and grammar of a language which helps 'the child rise to a higher level of speech development' (1962, p.101). He further argued that writing demands abstraction of two kinds. The first is at the level of psychological processes.

> Written speech is a separate linguistic function, differing from oral speech in both structure and mode of functioning. Even its minimal development requires a high level of abstraction. It is speech in thought and image only, lacking the musical, expressive, intonational qualities of oral speech. In learning to write, the child must disengage himself [*sic*] from the sensory aspect of speech and replace words by images of words. Speech that is merely imagined and that requires symbolization of the sound image in written signs (i.e. a second degree of symbolization) naturally must be as much harder than oral speech for the child as algebra is harder than arthmetic. (Vygotsky, 1962, pp.98–99)

The second kind of abstraction arises from the fact that writing, unlike speech, cannot be part of a dynamic social situation such as a conversation and therefore has to be more consciously directed by the child.

> The motives for writing are more abstract, more intellectualized, further removed from immediate needs. In written speech we are obliged

to create the situation, to represent it to ourselves. This demands detachment from the actual situation. (Vygotsky, 1962, p.99)

The influence of reading has been explored by Margaret Donaldson (1978). She has argued that 'the early mastery of reading is even more important than it is commonly taken to be' because, from the standpoint of psychological theory, children's thinking develops when something gives them pause and they have to consider more than one possibility. She suggests that,

> the lasting character of the print means that there is time to stop and think, so that the child has a chance to consider possibilities — a chance of a kind which he [sic] may never have had before. (Donaldson, 1978, p.95)

There may well be other ways in which this kind of thinking could be developed but literacy is clearly one, very powerful, way.

Inequalities in Literacy and the Importance of the Home

Despite the evident importance of literacy, there are wide variations in the literacy abilities of children and adults. Reference has already been made to adults with literacy difficulties. They constitute a small but significant minority in Britain (and in comparable societies). Exact numbers are difficult to determine since there are methodological problems in defining illiteracy and in surveying and assessing adults' competence.

Research in the United States has sought to determine levels of literacy in terms of performance criteria. The National Adult Literacy Survey sampled around 13,600 adults and distinguished five levels of literacy (Kirsch *et al.*, 1993). It found that almost a quarter had skills in the lowest level of proficiencies and were unable to perform 'quite limited' reading and writing tasks. The study also showed a huge variation in literacy skills related to quality of life and employment opportunities.

Testing adults may not be the best way to determine literacy levels since literacy ability is a relative concept and what matters is the individual's ability to cope with the demands they experience in society. The alternative is to use adults' self-reports of literacy difficulties (although that is open to criticism on the grounds that it relies on individuals' own judgments about their abilities and various factors such as their job, their aspirations or their understanding of the interview questions could lead to either an overestimate or an underestimate of 'true' literacy levels).

The approach of simply asking adults whether they have had difficulties with reading or writing since leaving school was taken in Britain in the fourth National Child Development Study follow-up study when a national sample of over 12,500 23-year-olds was interviewed (ALBSU, 1987). Around 10 per cent of the adults reported difficulties with reading, writing or spelling. Of these, about half had difficulties just with writing (including spelling) but not with reading; the others had difficulties with both. Some of their comments on their situation were quoted earlier in this chapter. Less than one in ten of those with difficulties had attended any kind of adult literacy course. Although some had had literacy difficulties at school and were in manual jobs, it is interesting that a significant number had not received any special help in school and were in non-manual jobs. In other words, the 'illiterate' on this definition did not conform to any easily identified stereotype. Although about a quarter reported that their literacy difficulties were in some way work-related, for most they were encountered in a wide range of contexts.

These findings have been replicated in a British study of a nationally representative sample of 1650 21-year-olds (Ekinsmyth and Bynner, 1994). The pattern of self-reported difficulties appears to be the same as in the 1987 study but this one also assessed the young people's performance on a set of tasks. It found that 5 per cent could not find a restaurant address from the *Yellow Pages*, 24 per cent could not locate basic information in a video recorder manual, and 48 per cent could not read advice about how to help someone suffering from hypothermia. Literacy scores based on such tasks were strongly related to family background, school attainment and employment history. The authors concluded,

> A picture emerges of the person lacking basic skills as being marginalised first in education and then in the peripheral unskilled regions of the labour market, typically with long spells of unemployment. (Ekinsmyth and Bynner, 1994, p.55)

Returning to the NCDS sample, a more recent study has shown the relation between parents' literacy and children's literacy. At age 33, by which time many of the adults were parents, a representative sample of families was studied as part of the fifth NCDS sweep (ALBSU, 1993). A reading test was given to 2617 children from 1761 families and their performance was analysed in relation to whether or not their parents reported having literacy difficulties. Some 4 per cent of children had parents with reading difficulties and 11 per cent had parents with writing or spelling difficulties. These children were much more likely to have poor reading test scores than were others. For example, 48 per cent of children of parents with reading difficulties were in the lowest quartile (compared, of course, to 25 per cent for the sample as a whole). If the parents also had a low income the likelihood of children being in the lowest quartile went up to 72 per cent. This correlation suggests that inequalities relate to *families* rather than just to adults or children.

Amongst children there is also considerable evidence of huge variation in literacy development linked to home factors. This will be dealt with in more detail in Chapter 3 when the case for parental involvement in the teaching of literacy will be considered. Evidence, for example, from NCDS surveys of children aged 7, 11 and 14 shows wide and growing differences between children from different social backgrounds (Davie *et al.*, 1972; Wedge and Prosser, 1973; Fogelman and Goldstein, 1976). At age 11 children from the most disadvantaged 6 per cent of households were an average of *three and a half years* behind others in reading test scores (Wedge and Prosser, 1973).

In summary, it is clear that literacy remains very unequally distributed in society and that it is strongly related to out-of-school factors, particularly home circumstances.

Literacy *for something*

Given that literacy is important culturally, personally and educationally, we may wish to do something about inequalities — specifically by focusing more on children's home experiences. Such action has to be part of a wider concern because increased literacy cannot be a goal in itself. Neither is it a guarantee of economic, political or personal progress.

The benefits of literacy — and the dangers of illiteracy — are often matters of official concern. In 1988 the European Commission argued that the 'persistence of illiteracy in industrialised countries' of the Community was 'a worrying social problem concerning a large number of the working population' (Commission of the European Communities, 1988). Against the background of attempts by the Community to establish itself as a competitive industrial and trading bloc, the Commission expressed concern about the 'social cost of illiteracy in our societies, in terms of manpower which can only be retrained with difficulty, in terms of unused potential'. An action research programme in 'the prevention and combating of illiteracy' was launched. At the same time, the United Nations was led to proclaim 1990 as 'International Literacy Year' on the grounds that illiteracy was linked to poverty, underdevelopment, child health and economic, social and cultural exclusion (UNESCO, 1988).

These views invite the metaphor of illiteracy as disease — something to be eradicated. Yet the fullest possible literacy will not be sufficient to bring about the changes sought unless there are also changes in other determining factors. Graff (1991) has shown that there is little historical justification for supposing that in the past increased literacy was associated with economic progress. In the future, literacy may, at best, be a necessary condition for certain kinds of development; it cannot possibly be a sufficient condition.

Literacy is often associated with radical political goals to do with demands for democratic rights and power. The fact that written language is such a powerful tool means that the question of who should be able to use it, and what they should use it for, has always been deeply political. The historical trend in most societies has been for literacy to spread from more powerful groups to the rest of the population. The least powerful are the last to become literate, and the kind of literacy they are expected to acquire may not extend to all uses of written language.

It has been argued that literacy is essential for political freedom (a 'necessary condition for liberty' to use George Bernard Shaw's phrase), for access to political ideas, and for the level of organization needed to bring about political change. However, here too what matters is not literacy in itself but its place in a wider political education.

In nineteenth-century Britain for example, working-class political aspirations included a concern with literacy as a part of universal education and universal suffrage. One of the leading Chartists, William Lovett, in 1841 made extremely detailed proposals for a method of teaching reading and writing. It was intended to replace learning 'by rote, without understanding' with a 'closer connection of words and things'. Crucially, however, this was coupled with a political vision of education for the working classes which went beyond 'the mere teaching of "reading, writing, and arithmetic" ' and which sought to remove 'the obstacles to their liberty and impediments to their happiness which ignorance still presents'. Lovett wanted to develop a certain kind of meaningful literacy because he believed it would enable the oppressed to understand what was being done to them.

> The fact of an insignificant portion of the people arrogating to themselves the political rights and powers of the whole, and persisting in making and enforcing such laws as are favourable to their own 'order', and inimical to the interests of the many, affords a strong argument in proof of the ignorance of those who submit to such injustice. (Lovett, 1841, in Simon, 1972, p.245)

In our own time there are well known examples from Latin America in the work of the Brazilian educator Paolo Freire (1970, 1972) and the Nicaraguan Literacy Crusade (Lankshear, 1987) of literacy campaigns. These too are examples of literacy for a purpose, however, that of the political struggle of oppressed groups. In the 1960s Freire developed a distinctive method of teaching literacy to adults (Brown, 1975). Exploiting the phonic regularities of written Portugese, the method was based on learning to read sixteen or so multisyllabic words which between them covered most of the grapheme–phoneme correspondences found in the language. Adults were shown how the words could be broken down into syllables which could then be recombined in various ways to form new words (or nonsense words). This technique, however, was subordinated to wider political and pedagogical values. The selection of the words came out of a long process of joint investigation between teachers and taught of 'themes' which were important in the lives of the taught. The words were highly charged (e.g. 'hunger', 'vote', 'illness', 'wealth') and were only introduced in their written form after their meanings had been extensively explored in discussion (with drawings and other representations as stimuli).

The important thing, from the point of view of libertarian education, is for men [*sic*] to come to feel like masters of their thinking by discussing the thinking and views of the world explicitly or implicitly manifest in their own suggestions and those of their comrades. Because this view of education starts with the conviction that it cannot present its own program but must search for this program dialogically with the people, it serves to introduce the pedagogy of the oppressed, in the elaboration of which the oppressed must participate. (Freire, 1970, p.118)

The point is that literacy by itself cannot guarantee liberty or any political progress. It can even make it easier to control people, as has been argued by Neil Postman:

It is probably true that in a highly complex society, one cannot be governed unless he [*sic*] can read forms, regulations, notices, catalogues, road signs, and the like. Thus, some minimal reading skill is necessary if you are to be 'good citizen', but 'good citizen' here means one who can follow the instructions of those who govern him. If you cannot read, you cannot be an obedient citizen. You are also a good citizen if you are an enthusiastic consumer. And so, some minimal reading competence is required if you are going to develop a keen interest in all the products that it is necessary for you to buy. If you do not read, you will be a relatively poor market. In order to be a good and loyal citizen, it is also necessary for you to believe in the myths and superstitions of your society. Therefore, a certain minimal reading skill is needed so that you can learn what these are, or have them reinforced. (Postman, 1970, p.246)

What this implies for parental involvement is that schools should be wary of promoting literacy as if it were self-evidently an end in itself. It is rather a means by which parents can reach goals that they may value for themselves or their children.

Brian Street has sought to distinguish what he terms 'autonomous' and 'ideological' models of literacy (Street, 1984). The 'autonomous' model embodies assumptions often made by educators and psychologists (that literacy alone provides certain cognitive benefits, that its development is unidirectional, that it is separable from schooling, and that it brings about economic, social and political progress). Street argues that this model overgeneralizes from one narrow, culture-specific literacy practice. The 'ideological' model recognizes that the meaning of literacy cannot be separated from the social institutions in which it is practised or the social processes whereby practitioners acquire it.

The actual examples of literacy in different societies that are available to us suggest that it is more often 'restrictive' and hegemonic, and concerned with instilling discipline and exercising social order. (Street, 1984, p.4)

One difficulty in understanding the political significance of literacy is that the vocabulary of literacy is sometimes hijacked for ideological purposes in order to disguise or legitimate processes of oppression or exclusion in society. If certain social groups are oppressed and if they are also largely illiterate (according to some concept of 'literacy') it may be convenient to explain their position as being *the result* of illiteracy. This is a more comforting explanation for social ills than accounts in terms, say, of racism, market forces or the needs of the rich. In this discourse, the term 'illiterate' serves as a substitute for 'unemployed', 'poor', 'black' or 'working-class'. The definition of illiteracy can be narrowed or widened as convenient. For example, in the United States, illiteracy is sometimes equated with 'high school dropout' thereby implying that a very large group of people face the difficulties which ought properly to be ascribed to only a few. To reinforce the point, there can be attempts to ameliorate the circumstances of such groups by token (and ultimately futile) attempts to raise literacy levels. Freire (1972) provides a blunt commentary on this.

> Merely teaching men [*sic*] to read and write does not work miracles;
> if there are not enough jobs for men able to work, teaching more men
> to read and write will not create them. (Freire, 1972, p.25)

In the United States, strands of the 'family literacy' movement (to be discussed in Chapter 7) have this character — poverty and unemployment are represented as problems caused by low literacy levels in certain communities and the proposed solution is a particular kind of literacy program.

Insofar as illiteracy serves as a justification for injustice, it may even be in the interests of ruling groups in society to perpetuate high levels of illiteracy in certain groups. This can be done by lower resourcing of literacy teaching (e.g. reduced funding for books, unfavourable teacher–pupil ratios), by overly rigid definitions of what is to count as literacy, and by biased or narrow forms of assessment.

It is not possible here to attempt to disentangle everything that makes literacy such a political issue. The point is that, in discussing the interrelations between literacy, home, school and society, one has to take care to avoid an uncritical formulation of what are problems and what are solutions. Literacy does have a potential for both oppression and liberation. The assumption underlying this book is that it is worth trying to provide as many children and adults as possible with the opportunity to use written language as fully as possible for purposes they value. It will not be assumed that, by itself, the ability to participate in any particular literacy activity is sufficient to secure any specific political goal. However, the *way* in which schools seek to involve parents in the teaching of literacy — in particular whether parents are treated as political agents or as technicians implementing a school progamme — may be of great political significance. It can be argued that parental involvement fails even in narrow terms if there is not also parental empowerment (Rasinski, 1989).

Different Forms of Literacy

The fact that literacy is embedded in culture means that it is likely to vary between cultures. This is not just a matter of variation in the particular written language or script being used or variation in subject matter. Of more significance is variation in the *uses* of that written language. Here we need to recognize that even within a country such as Britain, and even amongst those inhabitants for whom English is a first language, there are different cultures and subcultures. They can be distinguished, for example, in terms of region, ethnicity, occupation and social class. In each case the potential uses for written language may be the same but the pattern of actual uses may differ markedly. For example, writing for publication (in books or newspapers) is more common in middle-class than in working-class culture. Writing of personal letters may not vary so much. Reading of novels may well vary, but reading for information may not.

One response to this is to argue that literacy is the ability to use written language — the actual uses that particular readers and writers have for it is another matter, which depends on a complex of social, economic and political factors. This view has its critics. Postman (1970) argued that reading is not a neutral 'skill' and cited Plato in support of his view that there is probably something intrinsic to the medium of written language that induces passivity in those who use it.

Colin Lankshear has also criticized the idea of the 'neutrality' of literacy, but on rather different grounds.

> I argue that literacy is the uses to which it is put and the conceptions which shape and reflect its actual use. Once this is admitted we do more than merely achieve relief from the gross reification of literacy involved in the literacy-as-a-neutral-skill-or-technology view. In addition, we are freed to ask a whole range of questions that we are effectively discouraged from asking if we assume that literacy is neutral. For we can now entertain the possibility that the forms reading and writing take in daily life are related to the wider operation of power and patterns of interest within society. (Lankshear, 1987, p.50)

He suggests, as does Street (1984), that there are many 'literacies'.

> There is no single, unitary referent for 'literacy'. Literacy is not the name for a finite technology, set of skills, or any other 'thing'. We

should recognize, rather, that there are many specific literacies, each comprising an identifiable set of socially constructed practices based upon print and organized around beliefs about how the skills of reading and writing may or, perhaps, should be used. (Lankshear, 1987, p.58)

The suggestion that there could be many literacies is a disturbing one for educators. Teacher training courses and textbooks rarely acknowledge it as a possibility or a problem. This is especially so perhaps in early childhood education where teachers have been drawn to individual psychological models of development more than have teachers of older students. Which literacy should we teach, and why? What if the child's home literacy is different from the school's literacy? There are certainly some fundamental problems here but, even if we accept that there are many different literacies, it does not follow that they are all *completely* different. Because there are many branches of literacy it does not follow that there is no tree. There may be significant overlaps between apparently different literacies or core processes common to many literacy activities, especially in the early stages of learning them.

The value of a socio-political perspective which posits different literacies is that it focuses attention on ways in which 'school literacy' may differ from, and may even be in conflict with, 'home literacy', 'community literacy' or 'workplace literacy'. For some families — specifically middle-class ones — there may be a high degree of congruence between home literacy, school literacy and workplace literacy but for other families school literacy may be far removed from that which they encounter at home or at work. This can give rise to some troublesome issues in involving parents in the teaching of literacy.

The problematic, even contentious, nature of current school literacy is often hidden and it is hard to imagine alternative conceptions of it. However, one way to appreciate the *constructed* nature of school literacy is to take an historical perspective. In the past, there were different conceptions about it. An interesting issue has been the teaching of writing, particularly for working-class children. For example, in the 1790s, Hannah Moore, an influential figure in the establishment of Sunday Schools for working-class children, is quoted by Brian Simon as insisting that they should not be taught to write at all. 'I allow of no writing for the poor. My object is not to make them fanatics, but to train up the lower classes in habits of industry and piety' (Simon, 1960, p.133). Simon also quotes Andrew Bell who became superintendent of the 'National Society' which promoted church schools for the poor. In 1805 Bell argued that children should be taught to read (the Bible) but he felt differently about writing: 'It is not proposed that the children of the poor be educated in an expensive manner, or even taught to write and to cypher' (Simon, 1960, p.133).

Later in the century, the state became involved in funding mass education for the working classes. In 1862 this led to the notorious 'Revised Code' which stipulated what level of attainment was required of children for a school to be

Table 1.1: *A nineteenth-century view of school literacy*

Standards required by the 'Revised Code' of 1862

STANDARD	READING	WRITING
I	Narrative in monosyllables.	Form on blackboard or slate, from dictation, letters, capital and small manuscript.
II	One of the narratives next in order after monosyllables in an elementary reading-book used in the school.	Copy in manuscript character a line of print.
III	A short paragraph from an elementary reading-book used in the school.	A sentence from the same paragraph slowly read once and then dictated in single words.
IV	A short paragraph from a more advanced reading-book used in the school.	A sentence slowly dictated once by a few words at a time, from the same book but not from the paragraph read.
V	A few lines of poetry from a reading-book used in the first class of the school.	A sentence slowly dictated once by a few words at a time, from a reading-book used in the first class of the school.
VI	A short ordinary paragraph in a newspaper or other modern narrative.	Another short ordinary paragraph in a newspaper or other modern narrative, slowly dictated by a few words at a time.

Source: Birchenough, 1914, pp.279–80.

funded. There were six levels or 'standards'. It can be seen from Table 1.1 that these were not very ambitious but what is striking from a late twentieth-century perspective is the fact that reading was seen as *oral reading*. Also, writing was conceived of as *writing from dictation*. The idea of pupils writing something of their own does not appear to have been valued. In fact it was many years before 'composition' was considered appropriate in the elementary school curriculum, and then at first only for older pupils (Birchenough, 1914).

Several generations on, there is again a national curriculum in England. Many would feel that the current version (DES, 1989) is not as restrictive as the last one at the end of the nineteenth century, but who can say how it will be regarded from a vantage point at the end of the twenty-first century? As I write, further changes to the national curriclum are in the air. A struggle is taking place between those who wish children to be taught phonic skills more explicitly and at an earlier age and those who would rather emphasize meaning and engagement in the early school years; between those who want older children to learn to appreciate certain texts in a national 'literary heritage' and those who prefer a wider choice. The only certain things about any changes that are made is that they will be decided politically and that they will not be permanent. The point is that what counts as school literacy at any particular time is not a given but is the result of social processes.

It follows that, for parents, the meaning of involvement in the teaching of literacy will vary according to whether it is *school* literacy they are being drawn into and the extent to which they are ready to accept that construction of literacy.

Rethinking School Practice

I can summarize the argument presented in this chapter in terms of a number of key points which might guide the development of schools' practice regarding children's literacy learning at home and the role of parents:

- Literacy really is important but only in the service of wider concerns, not for its own sake.
- Literacy is ultimately about the communication of meaning, not simply the perceptual and motor skills that may be required in particular reading and writing systems.
- Literacy abilities of adults and children are unevenly distributed in society.
- Children's literacy is shaped by out-of-school factors, particularly learning in the home.
- School literacy may differ from other forms of literacy in the home, community and workplace that deserve to be taken seriously.
- Current conceptions of school literacy, and the teaching of literacy, differ from those in the past, and are likely to differ again from those in the future.

In the next chapter an historical perspective will be taken to explore how schools' practice towards parents in the teaching of literacy has changed over the years.

Chapter 2

From Exclusion to Involvement

Until quite recently the dominant practice in literacy teaching in England was one of parental *exclusion*. Even now, the widely heard rhetoric of 'home–school cooperation' and 'partnership with parents' is not always matched by real involvement in practice. The deep structure of many schools' relationship with parents remains closer to exclusion.

The exclusion of parents has rarely been planned or deliberate, and most teachers in infant, first and primary schools have not thought of it in that way. Nevertheless most parents realize that they have virtually no part in how schools teach their children to read or write. Indeed, often, they have only the vaguest ideas, gleaned from what their children can tell them, about how that teaching is carried out.

This is curious since most parents do involve themselves in teaching the beginnings of literacy before children go to school (sometimes even producing competent readers at school entry). After children start school, parents may well continue to help with reading although they often feel that their contribution is separate from, and perhaps less important than, what teachers do in class. It is worth exploring how teachers and parents came to adopt these roles and to what extent they may be changing.

Reasons for Exclusion

There are many factors that have combined to exclude parents from the teaching of their children. First, it is worth recalling that the present system of mass schooling in England was introduced only four or five generations ago, with the specific design of taking children away from parents in order to educate them in separate institutions. At that time many parents were illiterate, children's attendance was compelled by law, and parents who did not send them to school could be brought before magistrates and fined. In the early years of the system many parents were in fact punished in this way. Histories usually dwell on the positive aspects of the 1870 Education Act and quite possibly many parents did value the new educational opportunities provided for their children. Many were poorly equipped to educate their children as a result of long hours of work and their own illiteracy or lack of academic experience.

Those who resisted the new measures may have done so from economic need for their children's labour or from ignorance rather than from reluctance to hand over their children's education to teachers. Nevertheless, the fact remains that the element of compulsion, and the elevation of school learning above home learning, meant that from the start the English system of education was characterized more by parental exclusion than by parental involvement.

There was no space for parents in the schools of the late nineteenth century. Indeed there was little enough space for the children. Classes were very large, classrooms were cramped and parents were kept at the playground gate. Teachers of the time resorted to techniques of mass instruction which appear, from the vantage point of the late twentieth century, to have often been heartless and of limited educational value. Contemporary accounts provide a picture of classes of young children, seated for long periods in galleries, learning by rote with very limited opportunities for individual work or dialogue with a teacher. For example, Tizard quotes from a Board of Education Inspector's report on an under 5 class.

> At a given signal, every child in the class begins calling out mysterious sounds: 'letter A, letter A', in a sing-song voice, or 'letter A says Ah, letter A says Ah' . . . The word 'stop' from the teacher, accompanied by an alarming motion of the pointer in her hand toward the class, reduces it to silence, the pointer then indicates a second hieroglyphic on the blackboard, which is followed by a second outburst, and the repetition of 'letter B, letter B'. (Tizard, 1977, p.201)

This is the complete opposite of how a child might be educated by a parent at home — in a small group, with freedom of movement, and with frequent opportunities for meaningful dialogue geared to the child's level of understanding.

One might think that in view of the difficulties faced by teachers at the time that they might have turned to parents for help, either through at-home or in-school learning activities, or both. However this would have been difficult for reasons that persist to the present day. Then, as now, teachers of young children were concerned to establish a professional identity (something which normally means laying claim to a distinctive body of knowledge). Even if they were uneasy about the teaching methods dictated by the nature of their schools, they would have been reluctant to admit openly that there were shortcomings that could be remedied by involving parents. To have done so would have undermined the legitimacy of the new compulsory system and their own role within it. At a time when industrial power appeared to promise so much, it would have been difficult to question the self-evident benefits of factories for the mind. Instead, they would have sought improvements within the school system through increased resources, more teachers, better training, longer schooling, and improved class teaching methods. This is roughly the course of action that has been pursued since.

Even today, primary teachers are under the pressure of having to teach too many children in too little space and with too little time to cover everything they are asked to do. One reason for parental exclusion in the teaching of reading is that parental involvement is seen as just one more thing to do, and a very time consuming one at that. It is difficult enough to work with a class of thirty or more children; to work with their parents as well seems to be asking too much. Energies appear to be better spent in getting one's classroom teaching right. We shall consider a different way of looking at this issue in later chapters. For the moment let us just recognize it as a possible reason for parental exclusion.

Another reason for parental exclusion is the professionalization of the teaching of literacy, particularly reading. No other area of primary education has spawned so many techniques, technical terms, theories, books, tests, teaching materials, fashions, or 'experts'. This partly reflects the importance of literacy in the curriculum and the need for teachers to develop methods but it also reflects theoretical complexity and confusion. If we had a complete theory of literacy we would have solved all the major problems of psychology, for it is a process which embraces perception, language, culture, meaning and understanding. This should make teachers of reading wary of dogmatic claims about how reading should be taught but in some cases it has encouraged them to think that those who know even less about reading, particularly parents, are not competent to teach it. Even the use of basic terms such as 'reading age' or 'decoding' can deceive teachers and parents into thinking that teachers have some exclusive professional knowledge without which parents cannot participate in the teaching of reading.

One example of how a 'professionalized' approach to the teaching of reading can exclude parents is the use of reading schemes. At first sight an integrated scheme of books graded for difficulty, through which children can progress stage by stage, appears an excellent teaching resource. In England, one HMI report described their use as 'universal' (DES, 1978) and a later study found that published schemes were used in more than 95 per cent of classes (DES, 1990). In North America, schemes ('basal programs') are even more elaborate and tightly controlled and, again, have been very widely used (Luke, 1988). Such curricula require teachers to control what the children read and their progression from one stage to the next. This implies regular monitoring, usually through hearing children in class. Such a system is bound to exclude parents because teachers are not likely to give them responsibility for deciding when children are ready for the next stage and neither parents nor their children have any part in choosing what is to be read. Also, as we shall see later, teachers do not generally encourage children to take school reading books home.

A particularly extreme form of parental exclusion occurred in the era of the i.t.a. (initial teaching alphabet). The Bullock Report estimated that in 1973 about 10 per cent of schools in England were using i.t.a. (DES, 1975). The proportion has considerably declined since then but where it persists parents are far less likely to teach their children at home with ordinary materials and they have no opportunity to use i.t.a. materials unless books are allowed home (although even then they could feel inhibited about getting involved). The point is that 'improving' teaching methods in ways that are inaccessible or incomprehensible to non-professionals has a cost — increased parental exclusion.

A professional approach to the teaching of reading can be taken too far, but that does not mean there is no need for teachers to be professional. Involving parents does require professional skills, albeit of a different kind to those required in class teaching. One reason for the extent of parental exclusion in schools is that teachers are poorly equipped professionally. Their initial training rarely deals seriously with practical or theoretical aspects of parental involvement (Atkin and Bastiani, 1988) and it is still quite possible for a teacher to qualify professionally without ever having met a parent in an educational context (Hannon and Welch, 1993). Once in post there are few in-service training opportunities to acquire skills. LEA policies, as transmitted by advisers and headteachers may not give much priority to work with parents. Teacher unions and associations may be wary about parental involvement, especially in the classroom. Overall, there is limited professional incentive to involve parents.

One final reason for exclusion should be mentioned. Schools are bound to find it difficult to reverse long held policies when there are very few models of involvement available for them to adopt. The prospect of involvement can easily be imagined as a series of problems to which there are no clear solutions. What might parents be invited to do? What changes are implied in the teacher's role? How is it possible to communicate between home and school? Is involvement practicable? Until the last few years there were no models of parental involvement to show how these problems might be overcome. Some now exist and one purpose of this book is to describe them, and to develop a critical appraisal of them, so that teachers and others concerned with primary schools can decide whether to continue with parental exclusion or move towards involvement.

Growth of Limited Involvement in the 1970s

A turning point for the involvement of parents in primary education in England was the publication of the Plowden Report (CACE, 1967). It recommended Parent Teacher Associations, freedom for parents to choose schools, home visiting by teachers, community schools, and pre-school contact with parents. A five-point minimum programme was suggested for all primary schools (a welcome for parents, meetings with teachers, open days, provision of information, and reports). If today many of its proposals seem rather modest, that is partly a mark of its success. Plowden shifted the terms of debate about parents. Outright parental exclusion was no longer respectable. Teachers who wanted to be closer to parents were encouraged to develop their practice. Even those who wanted to keep parents at arm's length came under pressure at least to *say* they were in favour of parental involvement. In this climate, there was a slow but steady growth of what might be termed 'limited involvement' of parents in the teaching of literacy. However, that involvement was in reading, not writing.

In the post-Plowden era involvement was seen mainly in terms of 'getting parents into school'. The objectives were not always entirely clear. There was probably a feeling that if parents were in school more, contributing in some way to the life of the school, they would understand better what the school was trying to do and they would have more positive attitudes towards it. Further, children, knowing their parents were sometimes in the school too, might not feel there was such a gap between home and classroom. The objectives were primarily social, although it was assumed that children's educational development would ultimately benefit from better home–school relations. There was little emphasis on parents being involved in working with their own children in school. Fears of children 'acting up' even led to parents being discouraged from working with their own children.

There are several reasons for describing this form of involvement as 'limited'. First, only a few parents were involved because most were not free to spend time in school during the day and, additionally, numbers were limited by space and the amount of time teachers could give to supporting and guiding parents. Second, parents were usually limited to the margins of the curriculum — washing paint pots rather than teaching maths — since teachers not unreasonably considered parents had not been trained for teaching, especially teaching children other than their own in groups. Third, parents had only the most limited influence on the curriculum itself which at that time continued to be defined, planned and implemented by teachers. Fourth, the impact of parents was limited because their unique advantages over teachers as educators of their own children in their own homes were not exploited. Instead, they were invited to work in the alien territory of the school — a less meaningful environment than the home for many — with children other than their own.

To describe this in-school involvement as limited is not to say that it is unimportant. It may be extremely important for those parents who do come into school and even if there are very few of them that is something to be valued. It may also be important in the lives, as well as the literacy development, of their children. Insofar as the parents function effectively as 'reading volunteers' there will be benefits for other children too, and teachers may be freed to concentrate their time on other work in class. Also, even parents who find it difficult to help in school may appreciate the fact that if they could get into school they would be welcomed by teachers.

Some schools did attempt, in this period, to involve parents at home. Written advice in school booklets and circulars pointed out ways in which parents could help children by reading stories to them, using the public library and hearing children read. In some cases school reading books were allowed home; in others children may have been actively encouraged to take them home but it is doubtful whether were any schools that took this so seriously as to ensure that all children took books home regularly and that all parents received support and encouragement to hear them read or otherwise share the books. However, the idea of involving parents in the teaching of writing was hardly considered at all.

Another development that had a bearing on parent involvement was the growth in community education. In 1973 the first purpose-built community primary school in England, Belfield Community School, Rochdale, was opened. Primary schools in other areas of the country were built or adapted for a community function; the thrust was at the LEA level. Coventry, for example, established a Community Education Project that operated across a number of primary schools. The term 'community education' tends to be used rather loosely to refer to a variety of broadly educational, overlapping approaches to work with children, teenagers, parents and other adults, usually in the poorer urban areas, and it can include very different activities, having practically nothing in common with each other. Nevertheless, in relation to the education of young children, a community education orientation usually means valuing what children can learn from their communities (including the home and family) as well as what they can learn from schools. This opens the way to involving parents in central parts of children's education such as learning to read. The Coventry Community Education Project encouraged parents in schools, reading workshops, homework, home visiting, lending libraries and bookshops (Pritchard and Rennie, 1978). Case studies of four community primary schools in different parts of the country reported in Rennie (1985) showed that each had some parental involvement in the teaching of reading. At Belfield Community School, the policy was to encourage parental involvement at all stages. Detailed guidance, contained in a booklet distributed to all parents at school entry, included very specific suggestions for pre-reading and early reading activities at home (e.g. reading stories to children, making books). Parents were told that children would be encouraged to take school books home and that it was hoped that parents would hear their children read (Belfield Community School, 1974). Compared to other schools studied by Hannon and Cuckle (1984) this community school's practice was unusually positive towards parents and it was later to provide the setting for a more intensive initiative.

Increased Involvement in the 1980s

In the 1980s there were a number of initiatives that changed thinking and practice about parental involvement. Interestingly, most of these were research-led. They will be dealt with more fully in later chapters but, for the purpose of charting the trend from exclusion to involvement, some key features can be noted.

Research by Jenny Hewison and Jack Tizard published in 1980 showed that an important factor in working-class children's reading attainment at age 7 was whether their parents had heard them read regularly in the early school years. This led to the enormously influential Haringey Project (Tizard *et al.*, 1982) in which researchers visited a group of parents at home and encouraged *all* of them to hear their children read books sent home from school. The research showed that, after two years, these children had better reading test scores than comparable children whose parents had not been involved in this way in the teaching of reading.

Before the Haringey experiment was completed or its results known, the Belfield Reading Project, prompted by Jack Tizard but designed and coordinated by Peter Hannon and Angela Jackson (Hannon and Jackson, 1987b), began at Belfield Community School, Rochdale. Like Haringey, Belfield tried to involve parents by regularly sending school reading books home and encouraging and supporting parents hearing their children read. It too influenced practice — not so much through its findings (which turned out to be less encouraging than Haringey's) but by being a visible example of involvement in practice.

Results from the Haringey Project began to attract interest nationally when the *Times Educational Supplement*, in January 1981, announced

> a report of a piece of action research which — if it gets the attention it deserves — could explode a whole area of primary practice and make way for a new and optimistic start.
>
> The message is simple. Involving parents systematically in teaching their children to read produced quite spectacular results.

Unfortunately, the Haringey Project itself was no longer running, having ended some three years previously and there was nothing for journalists or teachers to see in action. However, the *Sunday Times* discovered that the Belfield Project was working on similar lines and published an extensive report, titled 'The Belfield Experiment', in March 1981. Unusually for an educational feature at that time, it appeared as an extensive front page article in the review section. The effect was dramatic. The Belfield Project became a topic of discussion in numerous infant and primary school staffrooms. Overnight it achieved national prominence, and in the public mind was credited with the successes of the Haringey Project, in effect becoming its dissemination phase. The project received a stream of enquiries and to deal with these, an explanatory booklet was produced later in the year (Jackson and Hannon, 1981). This fuelled further interest, for the booklet was sold out and reprinted several times. Many schools used it as a blueprint for developing similar programmes of parent involvement.

Meanwhile, in London, another initiative was underway. Known as PACT (Parents, Children and Teachers), it was an attempt to encourage and support primary schools in Hackney and elsewhere in the Inner London Education

Authority area to involve parents in hearing their children read at home (Griffiths and Hamilton, 1984). Unlike Haringey and Belfield there was no very precise research focus and it is not easy to say exactly what was done, with how many parents, in how many schools (Griffiths and King, 1985). However, the idea of PACT was certainly well-promoted and it succeeded in increasing interest in this form of parent involvement.

There were many similar initiatives throughout the 1980s. Some succeeded in changing the involvement of many parents over a long period of time; others were relatively superficial. Some sought publicity; others worked quietly. By the end of the decade most schools knew that getting parents to hear children read at home was a form of parental involvement to be taken seriously and many had taken steps to increase it.

These schemes had a fairly 'open' approach to how parents should hear children read. They gave parents general advice to hear their children read in a relatively unstructured way, for example to sit close to the child, not to criticize 'mistakes' or to have the TV on, to talk about stories and to make the activity enjoyable. However, in the 1980s some more 'prescriptive' approaches emerged and had a major impact on thinking and practice. These were mainly directed at older, failing readers rather than all (younger) children. They will be dealt with in more detail in Chapter 7.

The best known prescriptive approach, 'paired reading', came to notice in the wake of the Haringey–Belfield publicity. The *Times Educational Supplement* in October 1981 stated,

> Backward readers can make up to a year's progress in just eight weeks by reading aloud with their parents, according to the dramatic results of a scheme devised by three Derbyshire educational psychologists.
>
> The results are the latest in a series of findings which show that systematically involving parents in teaching their children pays startling dividends.

Details were later reported by Roger Bushell, Andy Miller and David Robson (1982). The procedure was not new but the publicity accorded to it was of a new level and this undoubtedly had a significant impact on practice. Paired reading was widely taken up by other educational psychologists and by special needs teachers. In 1983 Kirklees LEA established a five-year Paired Reading Project led by Keith Topping, an educational psychologist. This had a major influence on later developments. The project provided schools in Kirklees with information about paired reading, training, consultation, finance and evaluation with the result that many ran their own projects. It also took a national role in promoting paired reading through publications, conferences, gaining media attention, and disseminating reports of projects and studies. This led to a substantial literature (Topping and Lindsay, 1991, 1992).

A number of variants of paired reading, and alternative procedures for parents to hear reading, also emerged in the 1980s. They included 'shared reading'

(Greening and Spencely, 1987), 'pause, prompt and praise' (McNaughton *et al.*, 1981), and some other prescriptive approaches (Young and Tyre, 1983; Bryans *et al.*, 1985). Although some of these procedures were quite promising none was as widely taken up as either the straightforward Haringey–Belfield hearing reading approach or the original version of paired reading.

The cumulative effect of all these initiatives was to change the climate for parental involvement. Many teachers were persuaded that *some* form of parental involvement in the teaching of reading was worthwhile even if they were unclear about the distinctions between 'home reading', 'parent listening', 'paired reading' and 'shared reading', and used these terms interchangeably.

Parental involvement in the teaching of reading changed in two ways in the 1980s; from allowing parents only an indirect role to allowing them a direct one, and from being school-focused to being home-focused. The two trends were mutually reinforcing because when the focus is on the home it is easier to acknowledge parents as teachers. However, once a direct role had been acknowledged in home-focused involvement, it became easier to think of allowing parents a more direct role in children's school learning too. Two key developments are worth mentioning. In *reading workshops* groups of parents were invited into school for regular sessions in which they worked with their own children on reading or reading-related activities with the support or guidance of teaching staff (e.g. Weinberger, 1983). In *family reading groups* parents and children came into school to read together and to share their reading experiences (Obrist, 1978; Beverton *et al.*, 1993).

At the same time there was a growth in parental involvement in other countries, certainly in the English-speaking world, although the forms of parental involvement which have developed have inevitably been shaped by the ways in which literacy is taught in particular countries and the ways in which schools interact with parents. In the United States, for example, there is generally a much more skills-based instructional approach to teaching reading which made direct forms of involvement rather difficult. One attempt to try a modified Haringey–Belfield approach was successfully implemented (Nurss *et al.*, 1993) but generally one finds schools that recognize the importance of involvement, preferring to enthuse parents about reading in general and getting them to help their children by creating opportunities at home to enjoy reading. On the other hand, in Australia, there has been interest in the Haringey–Belfield form of involvement and developments on similar lines. In New Zealand there have been several projects based on the 'pause, prompt and praise' approach.

The 1980s will be seen as a crucial decade in the acceptance and growth of parental involvement. However, two important limitations should be borne in mind. First, most involvement did not concern the teaching of literacy as a whole but only the teaching of reading, and frequently it was further restricted to parents hearing the reading of young (or failing) readers. Second, although involvement certainly began to be taken seriously in that period, the extent of its growth remains open to question.

How Far Has Involvement Gone?

There have been a number of surveys over the years that give us some idea about trends in parental involvement. They do indicate an increase but of limited forms of involvement. They also show how far parents have *not* been involved in the teaching of literacy, that is, the persistence of exclusion. Sometimes what researchers have not looked for is almost as interesting as their actual findings. For example, home-focused involvement has not received as much attention as school-focused involvement. Involvement in the teaching of writing, as opposed to the teaching of reading has scarcely been considered at all.

In the 1960s a survey was commissioned by the Plowden Committee (CACE, 1967). Some 3000 parents, in a carefully drawn national sample, were asked for their views about primary education. The concept of parent involvement explored in the survey was a comparatively limited one, restricted mainly to the kinds of contacts parents had with schools (open evenings, talks with teachers, fund raising events) but one or two questions did touch on the parents' role in the teaching of literacy. One indicator of a school's readiness to involve parents in the early stages of reading is whether or not school books ever go home with children. Parents were asked whether their child borrowed books from school — over half the children in top infants did not do so. This survey did not reveal how often, or how many, books were brought home so it is possible that in cases where it did happen it was quite rare. Interestingly, younger children who might have benefited most from parental input were actually less likely to bring school books home than were older children who had mastered the basics of reading.

In the 1970s Her Majesty's Inspectors (HMI) in England carried out a detailed survey of a national sample of over 500 primary schools (DES, 1978). In their review of the primary curriculum, parental involvement at home was not mentioned once. Some parents helped in school but the numbers were quite small. Most classes had no parents helping. Parents were found in about one-third of 7-year-olds' classes but, typically, only two parents a week visited the class and the most common forms of involvement concerned children's welfare, including supervision on visits. Involvement with children's learning, which took the form of hearing children read or assisting with practical subjects, occurred in only about one in five classes of 7-year-olds (and far less often in classes of older children). So the general picture was one of very little school-focused involvement, and home-focused involvement so rare that in this report the inspectors did not even discuss it. In a later survey of first schools the inspectors did consider the question of home use of school reading books (DES, 1982). They noted that in many schools pupils were allowed to borrow books to take home but they commented, 'sadly it was exceptional to find active encouragement for children to borrow both library books and other books from the age of 5.'

In 1977 a major study of parental involvement in primary schools was carried out by Richard Cyster, Philip Clift and Sandra Battle at the National Foundation for Educational Research (Cyster *et al.*, 1980). The NFER research included a survey in which a national sample of almost 1700 primary schools was surveyed by sending a lengthy postal questionnaire to headteachers. The questionnaire had been developed after extensive consultations with teachers and others concerned with parental involvement. There was a good response from schools, with over 80 per cent completing and returning the question-naires. The research also included case studies of selected schools and parent interviews. At the time this was the most comprehensive study ever under-taken of how schools involved parents in the primary years but, again, it revealed comparatively little parental involvement in the teaching of literacy.

It was found that, in relation to reading, parents helped in school libraries, covering books, etc., in 29 per cent of schools, and heard children read under the supervision of a teacher in 26 per cent of schools. Home visits by teachers (which might conceivably have related to reading) occurred in 20 per cent of schools, but little was reported about their purpose. These figures relate to schools, not parents, so that even in schools where parents were said to be involved it may have concerned only a small proportion of parents. Again, in this study, the concept of parental involvement adopted appears to have been one of parents coming into school to be involved in school-focused involve-ment. The idea of parental involvement in children's learning experiences at home — home-focused involvement — was not explored. This is a revealing omission but it would be unfair to lay the entire blame for it on the research-ers. Their view of involvement was formed in consultation with teachers and reflects the dominant view, even in schools which were noted for involving parents, and shared by HMI in their survey, that parental involvement means bringing parents into schools.

In the 1980s another NFER national study of parental involvement (Jowett and Baginsky, 1988) went some way towards correcting this omission. It rec-ognized that involvement could include 'involving parents directly in the cur-riculum with their own children at home or in school' (p.38). Unfortunately the survey was conducted at the level of local education authorities rather than at the level of schools, classes or pupils. Therefore, although well over 90 per cent of authorities reported parental involvement in reading in their areas, it is difficult to know what proportion of parents this meant. About half the authorities said that they had a 'substantial number' of schools with 'home–school reading of some kind' but this tells us nothing about how many parents in how many schools were or were not seriously involved. Nothing was re-ported about involvement in the teaching of writing. The survey is therefore not all that helpful in indicating the extent of parental involvement in the teaching of literacy. However, on the question of trends there was one inter-esting finding — most involvement was reported to have developed since 1980.

In 1984 Barry Stierer at the University of London undertook a national survey of 500 primary schools which concentrated particularly on the involvement of parents in the teaching of reading (Stierer, 1985). He found signs of an increase in school-based parental involvement since the first NFER survey seven years earlier. Stierer did not set out to investigate the extent of home-focused parental involvement although, unlike most earlier investigators, he did recognize its existence and importance. Headteachers of 45 per cent of schools said that parents helped and, as the help nearly always included hearing children read, this can be considered an increase on the 26 per cent found in the NFER survey. However, this survey did provide information on the proportion of parents involved. It appeared low. Even in classes where parents helped, the average per class was only 2.5. In other words, the great majority of parents were not involved in this way. Furthermore, a third of headteachers reported that parents, as a matter of principle, did not work with their own child.

One indication of a school's attitude to home-focused parental involvement is its willingness to allow school books to go home with children and its attitude to encouraging parents to help their children by hearing them read the books used by teachers in school. There are methodological difficulties in determining the exact nature — the deep structure — of school practice in this area. One cannot simply post questionnaires to headteachers or principals and expect their answers to give a full picture, particularly concerning what happens at the classroom level or in individual parent–teacher contacts. For example a head might report having a policy of sending reading materials home and of encouraging parents to hear children read but, of itself, this does not mean it happens on a significant scale (although such an attitude may be a precondition for it to happen at all). To find out what really happens one has to probe further and discover the policies of individual class teachers which do not always accord with those of their heads. Even then one could find individual teachers in favour of sending books home but overestimating the frequency with which it happens. Further probing might involve looking at whether records are kept by teachers, and indeed whether any monitoring of home reading is carried out at all. Finally one might go on to question children and parents about what happens.

If such methods are necessary to gain a true picture of the deep structure of school practice it suggests that one should look at a small number of cases in depth rather than try to cover too large a sample at a surface level. One research study attempted to do this by looking at just sixteen schools and focusing on one age level, children aged 6 to 7 years in the top infants year (Hannon and Cuckle, 1984). Headteachers were interviewed, and so were all teachers of 7-year-olds and a random sample of children from their classes.

Several interesting findings emerged. It was clear that headteachers and teachers recognized the importance of parents in children's reading development and several said that they had a close relationship with parents. It was also clear, however, that many were reluctant to involve parents in the *teaching* of reading. At one extreme were two headteachers who said they preferred parents to let schools get on with the job of teaching. Others stressed the difficulties of over-anxious 'pushy' parents or said that some were 'incapable' of helping their children. Yet, according to the children, nearly all of them were reading at home — most to parents or siblings. When staff were asked about sending school reading books home and encouraging parents to hear their children read it became clear that this was going too far. Schools generally favoured *alternative*, less direct forms of involvement such as parents reading *to* their children or helping them learn words specified by class teachers. There was a series of factors which reduced the likelihood of school books going home (heads not allowing it, class teachers not allowing it, having reservations about it, or not monitoring it). From what children said too there was confirmation that only a small proportion used school books at home.

A study carried out a little later in London by researchers at the Thomas Coram Research Unit indicated that teachers were a little readier to accept parents hearing reading at home but they still had considerable reservations about parents (Farquhar *et al.*, 1985). There were thirty reception class teachers in the study, from thirty schools in disadvantaged working-class areas. The researchers reached this conclusion:

> Most teachers place clear restrictions on the sorts of academic-related activities which they feel are appropriate for parents to engage in with their children at home. The activities they favour are those of encouraging general language development, prior to school and listening to children read, once they have started school. Moreover, teachers have low expectations concerning the number of parents who will engage in these particular activities. (Farquhar *et al.*, 1985, p.21)

By the end of the 1980s, there was some evidence, in a national survey of 120 schools carried out by HMI (DES, 1990), that parental involvement had increased somewhat. Amongst other findings this report stated that some 40 per cent of schools had developed 'impressive' home–school cooperation including such activities as curriculum meetings, home visits, booklets, videos, demonstrations of reading approaches, open days, book weeks, book fairs, school bookshops and parent lending libraries with books about reading. Many teachers were said to maintain a written dialogue with parents about children's progress which formed part of children's reading records. On the other hand, the inspectors observed that arrangements for children to take books home sometimes broke down, especially for the children most in need, They noted that, 'sometimes schemes began well in the nursery or reception class but petered out too quickly as parents or teachers found the continuing commitment irksome'.

In general, a picture of limited involvement of relatively few parents emerges from these studies. Sometimes researchers appear to have had a somewhat limited conception of involvement too (school-focused, and related only to reading). While it is possible that they might have overlooked what goes on, it is more likely that they reflect accurately a consensus about the range of practices to be found in schools.

How Much Support Has There Been for Involvement?

There has not been a great deal of official encouragement for parental involvement in the teaching of literacy. Although the Plowden Report (CACE, 1967) was influential in establishing the general importance of parents in primary education, in relation to involving them more directly in the teaching of their children, the Committee made no specific recommendations. It did list some examples of good practice which included one school where children were being sent home with difficult school work so that a parent might help them, and others where parents were encouraged to hear their children read. The emphasis in Plowden was on informing parents about the work of schools and establishing better social contacts between home and school rather than seeing parents as teachers too.

There was an opportunity a few years later to develop Plowden's ideas when the Bullock Committee reported on the teaching of language, including reading, in schools and how current practice might be improved (DES, 1975). However, the report concerned itself mostly with what children learn in school. Parental involvement was seen in terms of how parents foster positive attitudes towards books and reading (e.g. by reading to children), particularly in the preschool years. The report talked of parents being 'helped to play their part in *preparing* the child for the process of learning to read' (p.99, emphasis added). It scarcely mentioned parents having a part in the process itself, except to point to the dangers by referring to parents 'whose efforts have been unsuccessful, or positively harmful' and by wondering 'how many children with severe reading disability received misguided teaching from over-anxious parents in the pre-school years?' (p.97). The Committee did state at one point that it believed parents had an extremely important part to play but, by stressing dangers and only discussing a preparatory role for parents, the implication in the report was that a certain amount of exclusion was proper.

Subsequent official statements about primary education did even less than Bullock to increase parental involvement. The teaching of literacy was seen as an entirely school-based, in-school process and the consequent parental exclusion was taken for granted. The HMI recommendations about the teaching of reading in *Primary Education in England* (DES, 1978) made no mention whatsoever of parents. In their report, *Education 5 to 9* (DES, 1982), the inspectors commented briefly on the desirability of children being able to borrow school books to take home but, surprisingly, there was no explicit recognition that this meant a role for parents.

The later HMI publication, *The Teaching and Learning of Reading in Primary Schools* (DES, 1990) did take things a little further. This report was produced in response to claims that national reading standards were declining.

In the course of rejecting the claims, the inspectors acknowledged that 'the quality and extent of parents' support for children's reading had a positive effect on their standards of reading' (p.12). There was implicit approval for involvement through previously mentioned activities such as curriculum meetings, home visits, booklets, videos, demonstrations of reading approaches, open days, book weeks, book fairs, school bookshops and parent lending libraries with books about reading, and for teachers maintaining a written dialogue with parents about children's reading progress. Yet, here again, a strong cautionary note was struck. The inspectors reported that some schemes 'tended only to be taken up by keen or over-anxious parents' and that in other schools 'teachers had a formidable task overcoming lack of interest on the part of parents'. They commented overall that

> Many schools demonstrated the benefits of enlisting the support of parents in helping the children to learn to read. However valuable that help may be, it cannot be assumed that all parents are well-placed or inclined to help their child with reading at home. The onus is upon the school to ensure that reading is taught effectively with or without the help of parents. For schools where, for one reason or another, parental support is lacking, particular attention and extra effort often have to be given to reading. Moreover, where parents assist with the reading, vigilance is needed to ensure that the programme does not rely too heavily on their help and unduly reduce the input of teachers. (DES, 1990, p.16)

While each part of this statement is unobjectionable — and it is certainly worth pointing out that a role for parents does not mean the end of the teacher's role — the overall tone is not exactly encouraging for parental involvement.

Support for involvement varies from place to place. Findings from the NFER survey in 1986 of all 108 local education authorities in England and Wales (Jowett and Baginsky, 1988) suggested that there was a spectrum of commitment to parent involvement in reading. At one extreme some authorities did not report such developments in their schools; at the other, were eight who said they had initiated large-scale named schemes designed to encourage home–school reading. Just over half of those replying claimed that a 'substantial number' of their schools were involved in home–school reading of some kind.

There are variations not only in the extent of parent involvement activity but in its nature too. In some areas special techniques such as paired reading predominate; in others it might be hearing children read. The explanation for this is to do with the change agents who promote one or other variant of involvement. Often they are educational psychologists concerned with the remediation, or sometimes the prevention, of reading difficulties by a specific treatment. In other cases an enthusiastic adviser may promote one kind of involvement. Sometimes the role of a university in establishing a research project influences developments locally.

Many schools embark on parental involvement without local prompting. A headteacher or teacher learns about something being done in another area and tries something similar in his or her own school. Here the role of the educational press in disseminating ideas has been very significant. Press reports of the effectiveness of schemes have often been grossly exaggerated to the dismay of those who have been cautious about claiming too much but to the satisfaction of those eager for favourable publicity. Difficulties usually arise over simplistic interpretations of test results. Nevertheless the effect of such reports has been to make people sit up, take notice, and do something.

There has also been a changing perception of parents in education that goes far beyond their involvement in the teaching process. Their roles as consumers of education and governors of schools, and as voters, has been taken more seriously at a time when client–professional and consumer–provider relations in many other areas of society such as health, housing and business are being revised. Legislation in 1981, 1986 and 1988 has also changed the formal position of parents in the educational system. All this has contributed to teachers seeing parents in a new way.

Teachers too are often parents and, when stepping into their professional role, do not lose all their awareness of parents' concern for their children and power to help them. As their own ideas as parents have evolved so have their attitudes to parents they meet in their work.

Underlying all other factors that explain the growth of involvement is the simple fact that many teachers welcome ideas that enable them to do their job better. Many have been quick to appreciate how their teaching could be improved by involving parents in the right way and they have been willing to accept the risks inherent in trying something new to achieve this. Some will have welcomed the chance to work with adults as well as children — whatever the rewards of spending most of the day with young children, concentrating on that alone does not make for a balanced or happy working life.

Making Sense of Different Approaches

Teachers cannot possibly adopt all the ways of involving parents that have been outlined in this chapter. How are they to identify the options? It is not just a question of shopping around for the 'best buy' as Topping (1986) has, perhaps ironically, suggested. One way of involving parents may be utterly different from another and the two may not be directly comparable any more than a consumers' guide could tell a shopper whether a can of baked beans is a 'better buy' than a toothbrush. It all depends on what you want. It is not even possible to make comparisons in terms of a single common measure of utility such as reading test gains because, as we shall find in Chapter 9, valid measures of the effects of different forms of involvement are often not

Table 2.1: Features of involvement

TARGET GROUP	What age range? All children or some? All parents or some?
OBJECTIVES	Which aspects of literacy? Other, non-literacy objectives?
DURATION	Weeks, months, years?
METHOD	Assumptions about literacy learning? Nature of parents' role? Focus of parents' involvement with children? Location for teachers' work with parents?
EVALUATION	Is there any? Linked to objectives? Evaluation design?

available or, if they are, different measures have been used for different forms of involvement.

In Chapter 11 I will suggest, in the light of currently available research, how some forms of involvement might be preferred in certain circumstances. Meanwhile, in order to understand the variation in forms of involvement — and therefore to which circumstances each might be suited — it is helpful to analyse them in terms of the *target group* of children at which they are aimed, their *objectives, duration, method,* (including *focus, location, model of literacy,* and *parent role*), and their method of *evaluation.*

The most important issue in relation to *target groups* is whether involvement is *selective* or *comprehensive.* It is selective, for example, if it is aimed at children with reading difficulties (however identified) but not at their peers. Certain kinds of parents might be selected too. A comprehensive approach includes all parents of children of a given age or class group without selection except perhaps in terms of the school where it is attempted. Another characteristic of a target group is its *age range* which could lie anywhere between nursery and secondary level. There is a relation between age range and whether there is a selective or comprehensive strategy, selection being more likely with older failing readers.

If one examines cases of involvement closely they often appear to have different *objectives.* Although most are concerned to improve children's reading they sometimes concern other aspects of literacy. They are occasionally undertaken to create better home–school relations or to change parents' or teachers' attitudes in some way. Schemes initiated at a local authority level may have various kinds of political objectives including the need to be seen doing something about a particular problem or the need to find a role for a psychological or remedial teaching service. Even if the objectives are confined to improving children's literacy it is well to be clear what this means in practice. It could mean improving children's attitudes to reading or enjoyment since these are fundamental aspects of development, however difficult they may be to measure. It could mean minimizing the number of children needing remedial provision or referral to psychological services. It could mean accelerating children's progression through reading scheme stages or national curriculum levels. Only rarely are objectives couched in terms of specific behaviours such as children's performance on a criterion-referenced or standardized reading test.

Schemes vary greatly in their *duration.* Some like the Haringey or Belfield projects last two or three years; others, like most paired reading schemes, run for a couple of months or even shorter periods. These are clearly very different forms of involvement. The long term schemes have to be deeply embedded in school practices and family life but the short ones require fewer changes. This makes them difficult to compare because it is not clear which period or end point should serve as the basis for comparisons. The problem is akin to comparing running a marathon to running over a 100-metre course.

There are even greater variations in the *methods* of involving parents. *Focus* and *location* are important. Is the focus to be children's literacy learning at home or in school? Is the teachers' work with the parents to be based at home or in school? What *model of literacy* development underlies the form of involvement? These can range from skills-focused behaviourist models to psycholinguistic or emergent literacy approaches and some rather atheoretical ones too. Methods vary in what is implied for the *parent's role.* Are parents involved as parents (with their own child) or as adult volunteers (working with other children)? Is their role central or peripheral to the learning process? Do those wishing to involve parents treat them as partners having some say in what is done or as technicians to be trained to implement a specific technique?

Finally, there are very different approaches to *evaluation.* Some forms of involvement are closely linked to evaluation procedures; others ignore the issue. Some cases of involvement are rigorously evaluated; others have been sloppily evaluated. The evaluation approach is often determined by what others have done before and may be poorly, if at all, linked to the objectives of involvement. Widely differing kinds of tests may be used (individual oral reading tests, silent group tests, word recognition tests), standardized, if at all, on varying populations. The lack of uniformity in testing presents a further difficulty in comparing the effectiveness of different forms of involvement.

When one considers the many varying features of different forms of involvement summarized in Table 2.1, it is clear that the combination and permutation of features is almost endless. Most have yet to be tried. Therefore, rather than think in terms of limited number of models of involvement, it may be more useful for teachers to think of choosing combinations of features.

Chapter 3

Understanding the Case for Involvement

Finding an appropriate form of parental involvement, and sustaining it, requires a clear understanding of why it is worthwhile. The case for involvement rests partly on there being no justification for exclusion but in this chapter I want to put forward more positive arguments. These are based on what is known about how children learn at home, particularly in the preschool years; how home factors influence literacy development; how parents already try to involve themselves; new thinking about the teaching of literacy; and the recognition that involvement is a good in itself. This leads on to a general theoretical framework for understanding work with parents.

The Myth of the 'Bad Parent'

Some teachers fear that if parents become involved they would do more harm than good and that it is safer, in the interests of children, to distance them from the teaching of literacy. If true, this would certainly justify exclusion but we are faced here with myth rather than reality.

What grounds are there for believing that large numbers of parents deal with their children so insensitively or hold such inappropriate views of literacy that, if involved, they would damage their children's development? The research evidence is non-existent. Myths, however, involve a grain of truth. Here it is the fact that most teachers, at some point in their careers, do encounter *some* parents whose attempts to teach reading or writing have probably been counter-productive, but this is a poor reason for excluding *all* parents. A few difficult cases should not be allowed to determine a general policy. Also, when such cases are examined closely it can turn out that there are deeper problems than methods of literacy instruction or that, in the context of a child's family, what happens in relation to literacy may not be as disastrous as it first appears to an outsider.

Even where it is clear that parents have taught badly, with bad results, it should be remembered that they probably did so *without* being involved by the school. Their misdirected efforts may be the result of lack of advice or support — a consequence of exclusion. When one examines the myth of the 'bad parent' it turns out to be an argument for involvement, not exclusion. But the myth is pervasive and its power should not be underestimated for it can lead well-meaning teachers to treat perfectly able parents with suspicion. This can even happen, revealingly, when the parents are themselves teachers. One teacher said at a professional gathering, 'Why is it that when I go to my daughter's school I'm treated like an idiot but when I get to the school where I work I'm the headteacher?'

For some parents a real difficulty in helping their children will be their own illiteracy. Generally that is no reason to exclude them for, even if they cannot read themselves, they may still be able to help by encouraging their children, talking about stories, responding to the sense of what children read, and providing opportunities for children's reading to develop. If they cannot write, they can still encourage their children to do so. This applies even if English is their second language. In practice, *total* illiteracy is rare in England and of course it is even rarer for *both* parents (and all other members of the household) to be totally illiterate. It is more common to find parents who have 'difficulties' with reading and writing. That means they have some literacy and may be able to help their children in the early stages of learning to read. In some cases parents may, on account of their own unhappy experiences, be highly motivated to help their children. Sometimes they are prompted to admit to their difficulties and seek tuition for themselves. Whether or not they do so, it is clear that the need is to support and advise them, rather than to exclude them.

Exclusion is not just a matter of teacher attitudes and behaviour. Parents have some responsibility too and can exclude themselves by not being sufficiently confident to take up or create opportunities for involvement or by communicating clumsily with teachers. Being professional, however, means taking a sympathetic view of parents and recognizing that some have anxieties, stemming from their own school days, which can make it difficult for them to communicate with teachers in a straightforward manner. It is professionals, by virtue of their institutional position, who have the greater power and responsibility for teacher–parent relations.

Learning in the Home

During their school years children learn a great deal but it is a great mistake to think that all of their learning occurs in school. Much learning, perhaps most, is at home. It is easy for teachers to underestimate the power of home learning and to overestimate the importance of in-school learning because that is what is most visible to them and that, traditionally, has been their professional concern.

Children learn a great deal before they even get to school. So they should, for the preschool period is a large part of a child's life (even for the oldest pupils in school the preschool years represent more than a quarter of a lifetime). Children's accomplishments in this period include learning to walk, to use and understand language, many vital social skills, and a store of information about their environment. Most of this learning takes place in and around the home, and their principal teachers are usually their parents. Even if preschool children attend a nursery or playgroup, such attendance usually only represents a very small proportion their waking hours.

Despite its importance, researchers have been slow to study home learning before school entry. This is partly because of methodological difficulties — it is much easier to observe preschool children out of the home, in nurseries or in artificial experimental settings (or wait until the children start school). Consequently we know more about the 'what' of learning — the ages at which preschool children can or cannot do certain things — than we know about the 'how' of learning in the home. Nevertheless there have been some useful studies. In one British study, researchers visited the homes of 165 preschool children, aged 3 to 4 years, and noted the children's activities during six one-hour periods spread over several days — a considerable undertaking (Davie *et al.*, 1984). They succeeded in documenting many activities in which children engaged, some of which were related to literacy development. For example, out of some fifty activities identified by the researchers, looking at books was one of the most frequently observed. Nearly all children (94 per cent) did it at least some of the time, often with adult participation. It occupied, on average, about 3 per cent of the children's waking day — less than the time spent watching television (9 per cent) but equivalent perhaps to twenty minutes or so per day, and therefore of some significance. However, knowing the types and frequencies of preschool children's home activities is only a start in understanding how they learn at home.

A more penetrating study was carried out in London by Barbara Tizard, Martin Hughes, Helen Carmichael and Gill Pinkerton at the Thomas Coram Research Unit (Tizard and Hughes, 1984). Their technique was to attach radio transmitter microphones to children so that samples of their conversations at home could be recorded and analysed. Thirty children, all 4-year-old girls from both middle-class and working-class homes, were studied and their language experiences at home were compared with their experiences in the nursery schools or classes that they also attended. The focus was children's language but, since language is a vehicle for a great deal of learning, this study has contributed to our understanding of children's learning. It also reveals the importance of the home environment that Tizard and Hughes explain in this way:

> As we started to study and analyse the transcripts, we became increasingly aware of how rich this environment was for all children. The conversations between the children and their mothers ranged freely over a variety of topics. The idea that children's interests were

restricted to play and TV was clearly untenable. At home the children discussed topics like work, the family births, growing up, and death; they talked with their mothers about things they had done together in the past, and their plans for the future; they puzzled over such diverse topics as the shape of roofs and chairs, the nature of Father Christmas, and whether the Queen wears curlers in bed. Many of these conversations took place during recognisably educational contexts — such as during play or while reading books — but many did not. A large number of the more fruitful conversations simply cropped up as the children and their mothers went about their afternoon's business at home — having lunch, planning shopping expeditions, feeding the baby and so on. (Tizard and Hughes, 1984, p.8)

Tizard and Hughes describe learning episodes in the children's conversations at home, in which the children actively sought information or ideas from mothers to further their understanding. Without tape recordings of conversations and analysis of transcripts, the importance of these episodes may not be fully recognized for they are easily lost in the stream of daily life. When the children attended nursery schools or classes they were in the company of many more children and only one or two adults. As might be expected, in the school environment, adult–child conversations were much fewer, briefer, and probably less fruitful.

The richness, depth and variety which characterised the home conversations was missing. So too was the sense of intellectual struggle, and of the real attempts to communicate being made on both sides. (Tizard and Hughes, 1984, p.9)

It is not clear whether nursery teachers can find ways to overcome the disadvantages of the school environment in this respect. What is clear, however, is that the home is an immensely powerful learning environment for the preschool child, and since the preschool period represents a significant proportion of any child's life it follows that teachers have to acknowledge that their influence is limited in comparison to that of parents.

It might be argued that after a child starts school teachers become more influential. This is obviously true to some extent, especially in relation to specialized areas of the secondary curriculum (although it is interesting that even then schools often rely on *home*work for children to make progress). Even for school children, time spent in school represents little more than a quarter of their waking lives and a great deal of learning must take place outside school hours. However, establishing the foundations of literacy is a matter primarily for the early years at school when the influence of the preschool period still looms large.

Table 3.1: Possible characteristics of children's learning at home and in school

Home learning	School learning
Shaped by interest and need.	Shaped by curricular objectives.
Often seems effortless.	Often seems to require effort.
Rarely formally assessed.	Often formally assessed.
Often spontaneous.	Timetabled.
Flexible duration.	Fixed duration.
Extended conversations possible.	Limited opportunities for conversation.
Natural problems.	Contrived problems.
May not encounter concepts in the easiest order for learning.	Planned progression through subject matter.
Special resources not usually available.	Supported by special resources.
Use of TV and print media often extensive and uncontrolled.	Use of audio-visual and printed materials subordinated to teaching objectives.
High adult–child ratio.	Low adult–child ratio.
Close and continuous relationships with few adults.	Distant and discontinuous relationships with many adults.
Adults as models.	Adults as instructors.
Recognition of children's achievements reflects many values.	Recognition of children's achievements reflects school objectives.
Vertical age group likely.	Horizontal age group likely.
Child sometimes in teaching role with younger children.	Very few opportunities for child to act as a teacher.
Opportunities vary with home background.	Opportunities more equal.
Accounts for much of the variation in school attainment.	Accounts for only a fraction of the variation in school attainment.

Taking a more general view of the relation between home learning and school learning, Hannon (1993) has suggested some possible characteristics of each (Table 3.1). There are even greater methodological obstacles to studying home learning in the later years than in the preschool years. In the absence of systematic research, one therefore has to be careful about generalization but it does seem plausible that there are many ways in which home learning could be much more powerful than school learning. For example, the scope for children satisfying their needs and interests, the relationships with adults, and the comparative lack of time constraints seem to point to the superiority of the home as a learning environment. On the other hand, the possibilities of planned curricular progression and the availability of special resources would seem to favour the school.

Home Factors in Early Literacy Development

Research into the nature of early literacy development has shown the importance of experiences before school and has emphasized the continuities between reading and so-called pre-reading experiences. Yetta Goodman (1980) has drawn attention to what she has termed the 'roots of literacy' in children's development. These include becoming aware of print as part of the environment, becoming aware of written language on its own (in books, letters, newspapers), grasping the functions and forms of writing, talking about written language, and learning to analyse and explain it (metalinguistic awareness). It is clear that children's reading must grow from roots such as these and it is also clear that these roots are nourished mainly in the home environment. When Goodman points out the importance of print in young children's environment, she is, by implication, referring to their *home* environment: 'I believe that the development of knowledge about print embedded in environmental settings is the beginning of reading development, which in most cases goes unnoticed' (Goodman, Y., 1986, p.7).

The term 'emergent literacy' has been used to describe the theoretical perspective taken in some studies (Teale and Sulzby, 1986; Hall, 1987). For example, a study of low-income families in San Diego reported by William Teale (1986) showed that preschool children participate in or observe a range of literacy activities in the home related to daily living (shopping, working, getting welfare, paying bills, travelling, obtaining services), entertainment (reading novels, TV guides, viewing text as part of TV programmes, doing crosswords), school (letters home, playing school, homework), parents' work (reading manuals, processing receipts, checking job advertisements), religion (reading the Bible, guides, pamphlets), interpersonal communication (letters, cards) and reading to keep up with things (newspapers, sport magazines). In addition, Teale found there was some storybook reading and activities undertaken to help children learn to read and write.

Shirley Brice Heath (1983) has shown that *what* children learn at home about literacy can very enormously according to the culture and values of their communities. She carried out a lengthy ethnographic study in the southern United States of two small neighbouring communities ('Trackton', black working-class; 'Roadville', white working-class) and found that their uses for literacy differed significantly from each other (and also from that of the 'mainstream' town community). For example, in Trackton children were more likely to be involved in literacy events with several participants; in Roadville, bedtime stories were more common. Heath showed how these differences were rooted deep in culture and in patterns of oral language use. Despite their preschool literacy experiences, children from both the working-class communities had difficulties with school literacy. The importance of this study goes far beyond what it tells us about literacy in the 1970s in two particular communities (which may no longer exist). It shows that children anywhere can learn about literacy before school and out-of-school, but they do not all learn the *same* literacy.

Several other studies point to the same conclusion (Goelman *et al.*, 1984; Taylor and Dorsey-Gaines, 1988). Even studies in the emergent literacy tradition which concentrate on young children's in-school learning, drawing attention to how much they know about literacy (e.g. Harste *et al.*, 1984), provide implicit evidence about how much the home contributes.

Another way to appreciate the importance of the home is to reflect on the relationship between oral language and written language. It is clear that one is dependent upon the other in the sense that the acquisition of written language nearly always depends on the prior acquisition of oral language. It is also clear (as Vygotsky and many others have pointed out) that there are profound differences between the oral and written language. However, what is of interest here is how children learn them, and the crucial role played by parents.

Children's early attempts at speech are generally taken seriously by parents who tolerate imprecision and errors and do their best to interpret what the child means — even at the babbling stage. Adults often structure situations to make it easy for children to understand and make themselves understood. Such assistance and encouragement is probably just as valuable in the development of reading and writing, from the stages of earliest 'scribbling' stage and puzzling out the meaning of texts. Children learn to understand speech by making sense of meaningful communication of varying levels of complexity in natural contexts so that although adults sometimes simplify their speech for children's sake, they do not always do so. Children do not usually have to undergo direct instruction in understanding speech. We do not have to expose them to utterances of graded complexity (by having a language programme of some kind) but it is often assumed that this is necessary for learning to read. One could characterize children's learning of spoken language as being 'on the job', in natural contexts, as required. It is reasonable to suppose that their learning to understand written language could be similarly facilitated in shared reading of books and other texts to achieve clearly understood and shared purposes such as the enjoyment of narrative. Margaret Meek has put it this way,

> Reading is whole-task learning right from the start. From first to last the child should be invited to behave like a reader, and those who want to help him [*sic*] should assume that he can learn, and will learn, just as happened when he began to talk . . . Learning to read in the early stages, like everything else a child has come to know, is an approximation of adult behaviour with genuine meaningful function. (Meek, 1982, p.24)

In so far as there are significant similarities between the development of children's spoken and written language it means taking seriously the fact that children could learn from a range of uncontrolled encounters with written language (many outside the school context), that such encounters need to be as meaningful as possible, and that parents and others at home are bound to have a key role in mediating them.

However, there are also differences between written and spoken language. For example, a writer cannot take it for granted that his or her reader will share the same context in the way that a speaker can often assume that a hearer does (indeed written language is more likely to be used when the two are not in the same context). This means that the character of written language often differs significantly from spoken language in being less context-dependent — more explicit and self-contained — than much speech (and is therefore rarely 'speech written down'). Children who are unfamiliar with using oral language in this way may find this difficult to grasp. Most of the different cultural uses of written language discussed in Chapter 1 have other, genre-specific, characteristics which can be hard to grasp if the user does not understand the purpose of the writing.

Finally, it is clear that in the normal development of spoken language the ability to produce speech is intimately connected with the ability to understand it. It may be just as helpful to recognize the links between reading and writing but it often happens that these two are treated as separate processes. The concept of *literacy* unites them. It will be apparent later that far less attention has been devoted to parental involvement in the teaching of writing than to involvement in the teaching of reading. Nevertheless, it is still helpful to think of involvement in literacy as a whole.

Home Factors in School Literacy Attainment

When we look more closely at children's literacy development after school entry the influence of the home, and therefore the need to take account of the role of parents, becomes more obvious. One of the clearest pieces of evidence on this point comes from the National Child Development Study (Davie *et al.*, 1972). In this research all the children born in one week in 1958 in Britain, numbering over 15,000, have been followed through from birth and studied at various ages. When the children were 7 years old, towards the end of their infant schooling, they were all tested on the Southgate Reading Test. Children who did relatively poorly on this test, the bottom 30 per cent, were studied more closely. It was found that the incidence of 'poor readers' according to this definition was related to a number of home factors, but none more so than social class. It can been seen from Figure 3.1 that children of fathers in social class IV (semi-skilled manual workers) were more than twice as likely to be poor readers than were those whose fathers were in class II (professional/technical jobs).

At the extremes of the social class distribution, between classes V and I, the discrepancy was much greater — a factor of six. If one considers *non*-readers rather than 'poor' readers the discrepancy was even more striking.

Figure 3.1: Proportions of 7 year-olds with 'poor' reading test scores, by social class

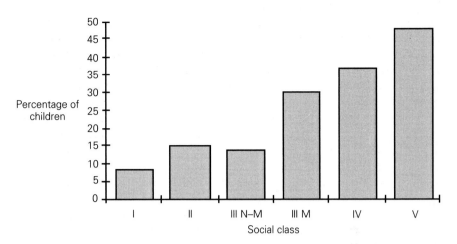

Source: Davie *et al.*, 1972, derived from Table A165, p.390.

Children in social class V were fifteen times more likely not to have learnt to read by age 7 than were children in class I.

These children were studied again at age 11. Wedge and Prosser (1973) looked at the children who came from particularly disadvantaged homes (coming from a large family, which also had low income and poor housing). About 6 per cent of children came into this category. In terms of reading test scores, they were an average of *three and a half years* behind other 11-year-olds.

The same kind of picture emerged from an earlier longitudinal study of 5000 children born in one week in 1946. Douglas (1964) found wide social class differences on an NFER reading test when the children were 8 years old. A later study in Nottingham by John and Elizabeth Newson found that 39 per cent of working-class 7-year-olds were said by parents to be non-readers — twice the proportion found in the middle class (Newson and Newson, 1977). In yet another study, Hannon and McNally (1986) compared the reading test scores of middle-class and working-class 7-year-olds and found a 27-point difference in mean scores — equivalent to more than two years' development.

Thus there is abundant evidence that children's reading attainment, at least as measured by reading tests, is strongly related to social class. Knowing a child's social class gives us only the crudest idea of his or her home background, however. It tells us something of the family's command of economic resources and the kinds of skills by which the parents, if they are employed, earn a living. It might suggest that the child is likely to have certain kinds of learning experiences or unlikely to have some other kinds, but it does not tell us anything about which learning experiences are critical, or why they should be critical.

It must be admitted that there are some methodological problems with research in this field. One, to be discussed more fully in Chapter 9, is that we must be careful about taking reading test scores at face value. It is likely that part of the social class differences in reading test performance might be due to test bias of one kind or another, and that more rigorous investigations of children's reading competence might reveal smaller differences (Hannon and McNally, 1986). This has happened in research into children's oral language where social class differences, once widely assumed, have tended to diminish as the quality of research has improved (Edwards, 1976; Wells, 1978; Tizard and Hughes, 1984). Therefore, to some extent, it must be a question of different kinds of literacy between the classes as well as more or less literacy.

Variations between homes in children's literacy experiences are not well understood yet. Further understanding will depend on detailed ethnographic studies of families from different social classes such as the one reported by Lareau (1989) but with more of a focus on literacy. Factors such as family income obviously play a part, not just in determining the availability of literacy materials in the home but also in creating opportunities to use literacy in consumption (shopping, visits). The nature of parents' work, and the extent to which it requires literacy, must be important too. These factors probably go some way towards explaining social class differences in attainment but the need is for studies that combine an interest in social class with a fuller analysis of literacy.

Parents Already Try to Involve Themselves

Many parents try to help their children with literacy but the extent of this help is not always recognized by the schools. One research study, at the preschool level, compared parents and teachers' perspectives on early literacy development (Hannon and James, 1990). Forty parents, in a random sample drawn from ten nursery classes, were interviewed at home and their children's teachers were interviewed in school about their respective roles in relation to children's reading and writing. Details of this study will be considered in the next chapter on teaching literacy with parents of preschool children but Hannon and James summarized their findings thus:

> What emerges from this study is that not only are parents interested in preschool literacy but that they claim to spend a great deal of time actually engaged in reading and writing activities with their children ... It was also apparent that they encouraged their children despite feeling that nursery teachers might disapprove. It seems that they provide books, writing materials, and a wide range of other materials designed to encourage their children's literacy development. It also seems that the children themselves are extremely interested and that

it is often they who initiate reading and writing sessions. (Hannon and James, 1990, p.268)

The London study reported by Farquhar *et al.* (1985), mentioned in the previous chapter, provided information about children just after school entry. Through interviews of over 200 parents of reception class children it found considerable evidence of parents involving themselves in children's school learning, including literacy but the children's teachers had low expectations of the parents' contribution.

Parents, on the other hand, whilst generally believing that schools and teachers make the greatest contributions to children's educational progress, nevertheless actively engage in many academic-related activities with their children, even before they start school. (Farquhar *et al.*, 1985, p.22)

Other studies have shown parents involved in the literacy learning of slightly older children. The Newsons found parents of seven-year-olds from every social class helping children's reading and they commented on the implications for teachers.

That over 80 per cent of our sample claimed in fact to have given help with reading would suggest that, in their varying ways, most parents see themselves as having some part to play in this basic aspect of their children's education, and yet this willingness is too often mis-channelled for lack of advice, encouragement and appreciation from those best qualified to give it. (Newson and Newson, 1977, p.150)

Even the Bullock Report, despite its anxieties about involving parents, recognized that the question was not whether to involve them in the teaching of reading but how to do so: 'There is, then, no doubt whatever of the value of parents' involvement in the early stages of reading. What needs careful thought is the *nature* of that involvement' (DES, 1975, p.97).

A particularly revealing study of the extent and value of parental help was carried out by Jenny Hewison and Jack Tizard (1980). They concentrated on studying 7-year-old children, all from working-class families in Dagenham. It is easy to overlook the fact that many working-class children go against the trend described earlier in this chapter and become good readers. What is it about these children or their home backgrounds that makes them do well?

Hewison and Tizard looked at a number of factors such as parents' attitudes to children's play and discipline, whether there was much conversation with the child, whether stories were read to them, how the children spent their leisure time, what attitudes parents had towards school, and so on. They also looked at mothers' language behaviour and at children's IQ scores. Most of these factors did matter to some extent (i.e. there were modest positive correlations

Figure 3.2: Relation between reading test attainment at age 7 and reported frequency of home reading for working-class children

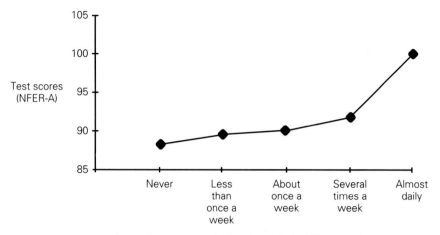

How often parents said they heard their children read

Source: Hannon, 1987, derived from Table 1, p.61.

with reading test scores). However one factor stood out above all others. It was whether or not mothers regularly heard their children read at home — not whether children had stories read to them, but whether they read to their mothers. About 90 per cent of children were said to have been heard to read at least occasionally in the early years of school but it was those being heard *regularly* at age 7 who appeared to have benefited most. About half the children were in this category and their reading test standardized scores were some fourteen points higher than those not heard regularly. Hewison and Tizard argued that this difference could not be adequately accounted for in terms of other factors such as parents' attitudes or child's IQ. These findings have been replicated elsewhere. Figure 3.2 shows clearly how in another sample of working-class 7-year-olds the frequency of being heard to read at home was strongly related to reading-test performance (Hannon, 1987).

What about middle-class parents? There is some evidence that they may be readier to hear their children read, and from an earlier age. A study by Liz Whitehurst in 1983 found that virtually all middle-class parents heard their children read regularly, although by age 7 this tended to be mainly with the poorer readers. The reading test scores for this sample were extremely high. The same study also found that the middle-class homes were very well supplied with children's books — collections of over 100 per child were common. This was also reported by the Newsons who found what they described as a 'massive class difference in book ownership' (Newson and Newson, 1977). Middle-class children in their study also had more comics bought for them and were twice as likely to belong to a public library.

Figure 3.3: Relation between reading materials in the home and reading test attainment (findings from the US National Assessment of Educational Progress)

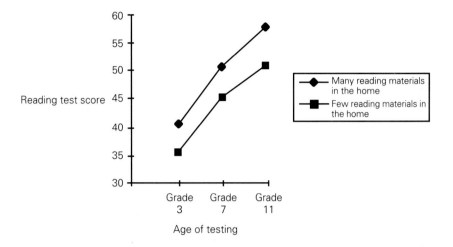

Source: Applebee *et al.*, 1988, derived from Table 5.5, p.51.

The association between lack of books in the home and school attainment was highlighted in England in the 1960s by the Plowden Report (CACE, 1967). However, more recent findings from the United States reported by Applebee *et al.* (1988) show the link particularly clearly. In the National Assessment of Educational Progress a nationally representative sample of 36,000 school pupils from three year levels — ages 9, 13 and 17 (Grades 3, 7, 11) — were tested for reading and placed on a single scale ranging from 0 to 100 with a sample mean of 50. Table 3.4 shows the mean scores of children at each age level according to how many reading materials they reported having at home. Those who had dictionaries, regular newspapers, encyclopedias, regular magazines and at least twenty-five books in the home were defined as having 'many' reading materials; those with three or less of these assets were defined as having 'few'.

Figure 3.3 not only shows that at each age level children with many resources had much higher reading test scores but also that 17-year-olds with 'few' resources were only at the same level as 13-year-olds with 'many' resources. There could be many factors (such as family income or parents' educational level) underlying the association but, on the surface at least, it suggests that home literacy resources might be worth several years of schooling.

These researches strengthen the case for involvement not just by showing that many parents are already involving themselves, and that their involvement is beneficial, but also by pointing to ways in which schools could improve children's opportunities. Parents already involved may need support and advice; the benefits enjoyed by some children whose parents involve themselves could be extended to all children; and schools may be able to do something to redress children's unequal access to books and other literacy materials.

Deprofessionalization of the Teaching of Literacy

The professionalization of the teaching of literacy was mentioned in Chapter 2 as a factor tending to exclude parents, but there is now a rethinking of what it means to be a good teacher in this field. There has always been some scepticism about the idea that only school teachers can teach. Twenty years ago Herbert Kohl argued,

> There is no reading problem. There are problem teachers and problem schools. Most people who fail to read in our society are victims of a fiercely competitive system of training that requires failure. If talking and walking were taught in most schools we might end up with as many mutes and cripples as we now have non-readers. However, learning to read is no more difficult than learning to walk or talk. The skill can be acquired in a natural and informal manner and in a variety of settings ranging from school to home to streets . . .
>
> Anyone who reads with a certain degree of competency can help others who read less well. This is the case regardless of age or previous educational training. However, most people in this culture are not accustomed to thinking of themselves as teachers. (Kohl, 1974, pp.9, 12)

For many years Frank Smith has been a severe critic of some ways of teaching of reading. In a celebrated chapter in his book, *Psycholinguistics and Reading* (1973) he listed 'Twelve easy ways to make learning to read difficult'. They included aiming for early mastery of the rules of reading, insisting that phonic skills are learnt and used, teaching letters or words one at a time, discouraging guessing, and ensuring children understand the seriousness of failure. These can be seen as aspects of an overprofessionalized approach.

Times may be changing however. New views about literacy development that emphasize parallels between the development of spoken language and the development of written language, the interconnectedness of reading and writing, and the value of what the child brings to the process of learning to read as well as what the teacher brings, have been gradually gaining ground. In North America this tends to be called a 'whole language' approach (Goodman, K., 1986); in Britain labels such as 'emergent literacy', 'real books' or the 'apprenticeship approach' (Waterland, 1985) have been used. The implications are similar. Structured schemes that require children to proceed through a series of stages, acquiring subskills in a fixed order, are being abandoned, modified or used more flexibly to make all reading and writing activities as meaningful as possible from the earliest stages.

This means a new position for parents. No longer need they be excluded by reading schemes or basal reading programs. Instead, teachers who wish to emphasize the meaningfulness of literacy activities have an extra incentive to enlist parents' support for it is in the home that children can most easily see the meanings of written language and where they can more easily enjoy it too.

The kind of learning presumed necessary by reading scheme proponents is very different from how children learn most things (including oral language) at home. The characteristics of home learning posited in Table 3.1 suggest that it does not consist of closely monitored and controlled progression through a fixed sequence of learning activities, carefully graded for difficulty. A disadvantage of the reading scheme approach is that the learning activities may not be as interesting and meaningful as those in the uncontrolled demands of home life (it can certainly lead to some very contrived and tedious stories). The home–school mismatch may be more disconcerting for children from some families than others depending on how close their home literacy experiences have been to school literacy.

Smith (1988) has used the metaphor of 'joining the literacy club' to characterize the social nature of literacy learning. He argues that children learn by joining a community of readers and writers who use literacy to accomplish real purposes. The established members of the club (including authors children encounter) draw the new members into their activities. They do not expect children to learn everything at once so they help them with things they cannot do in the confident expectation that eventually they will be able to join in all club activities. He suggests that this is the only way children can learn effectively, there being 'no evidence that any child ever learned to read by simply being subjected to a program of systematic instruction'. The metaphor is compelling but not all the educational implications are followed through. Smith urges teachers 'to ensure that clubs exist and that no child is excluded from them' but suggests only that they do this by providing a wider range of *classroom* activities. What is missing is any consideration of what teachers could do to promote out-of-school club activities in favourable settings such as the home. Parents and others in families are in a very powerful position to initiate new members into the club but they may need support to do this confidently and effectively.

The National Curriculum

In England, the teaching of literacy is being affected by the national curriculum with its programmes of study and attainment targets in English (DES, 1989). All children now entering school are subject to these provisions from age 5 to 16. To an extent these reflect some of the new ideas about literacy development discussed in this chapter but revisions to the national curriculum are now being proposed that would give much more emphasis in the early years to the teaching of phonic skills, spelling and punctuation (DFE, 1993). Whatever happens, there are implications for parental involvement.

The definition of literacy enshrined in the national curriculum orders will have implications for parental involvement. For example, the emphases given to speaking 'standard English', to learning and applying phonic rules in reading, to early learning of spelling and punctuation, or to appreciating a prescribed 'literary heritage' could serve either to widen, or to close, the gap between the literacies of the home and the school. Pressures to reach certain attainment targets could mean that teachers have less time and energy for home–school collaboration (e.g. for promoting children's enjoyment of books that may not be directly assessed) or that they will be led to enlist parents' help in reaching the targets (e.g. by sending home phonic skills exercises).

Parents are going to know more than ever before about what schools are trying to achieve for their children, and at what ages. They will also know more about whether the schools are succeeding, for by the age of 7, if not before, they will all be told what level their child has reached. This may increase parents' interest in the teaching of reading and writing and their desire to be involved, especially if there is the slightest suggestion that their children are behind. They are increasingly likely to turn to teachers and ask, 'What can I do?' Schools too are increasingly likely to turn to parents for help because the school's success, or lack of it, in getting as many children as possible to the appropriate level is going to be more widely known than ever. It will be in schools' interests to have the best possible way of teaching literacy and the widest possible understanding what it is trying to achieve. Many will conclude that it is better to have parents as allies rather than as critics.

Parents' Concern for their Children

There is one further, simple argument for involving parents in the teaching of literacy. Most parents love their children. The word 'love' does not figure prominently in the vocabulary of educational researchers but it refers to something fundamental. Most parents find involvement in their child's development, whether in literacy or other areas, *intrinsically* rewarding and fulfilling. This, after all, is one reason why they became parents.

Two implications follow. First, parents are a highly motivated teaching force and schools should not allow their potential to be wasted. Second, one does not really need to justify parental involvement in any other terms. It is not just a means to an end; it is already an end — a good — in itself.

A Theoretical Framework

Any attempt to involve parents in the teaching of literacy should have some theory, however modest, to help understand what is important about the parent's

Figure 3.4: What parents can provide for children's literacy development

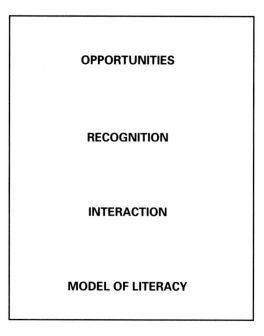

OPPORTUNITIES

RECOGNITION

INTERACTION

MODEL OF LITERACY

role, what experiences are likely to assist children's literacy development, and, broadly, what ways of working with parents should be considered. The arguments reviewed so far not only point to the necessity of schools working with parents but also provide some pointers about how it could be done.

The importance of the parent's role can be understood in terms of four things they can provide for developing readers and writers: *opportunities* for learning, *recognition* of the child's achievements, *interaction* around literacy activities, and a *model* of literacy (Figure 3.4). Some parents probably provide these more consciously, more meaningfully and more frequently than others.

In the early years, parents can provide vital learning *opportunities*: by resourcing children's drawing or scribbling activities; by encouraging their sociodramatic play; by exposing them to, and helping them interpret, environmental print; by teaching nursery rhymes that aid speech segmentation and phonological awareness; by sharing storybooks and other written materials; and by enabling children to participate in visits, trips or holidays that provide further literacy demands and opportunities. Parents can provide unique encouragement for children in their *recognition* and valuing of children's early achievements in, for example, handling books, reading, understanding logos, and writing. They need to *interact* with children — supporting, explaining, and challenging them to move on from what they know about literacy to do more. An important way of doing this is to involve children in real literacy tasks in which they can make a meaningful contribution (e.g. adding their 'name' to a greetings card, turning the pages of a book) thereby enabling to do today with an adult what tomorrow they will be able to do independently. Some parents deliberately teach their children some aspects of literacy. The extent of such help is gradually being revealed by research (Farquhar *et al.*, 1985; Hall *et al.*, 1989; Hannon and James, 1990). Finally parents act as powerful *models* if and when children see them using literacy, for example, in reading newspapers for information or enjoyment; writing notes or shopping lists; using print to find things out, to follow instructions; or to earn a living, for example, by bringing work home.

In the later years, parents can provide the same things but possibly in different ways. Providing literacy *opportunities* may mean facilitating children's use of libraries or creating reading time for them (for example, by limiting TV viewing). It may mean providing resources such as dictionaries, encyclopedias, magazines, newspapers, books, writing material, or even computers. *Recognition* of achievement means appreciating children's reading and writing more difficult texts at home and in school. Appropriate *interaction* in the form of talking about books, newspaper articles or writing tasks may not be as intense as in the early years but may still be very significant. As in the early years, it could take the form of direct instruction. Providing a *model* of literacy goes beyond merely being seen to read and write to a clearer demonstration of how these activities are linked to a wide range of adult purposes in the home, community and workplace.

It is also helpful, for practical reasons, to distinguish the three strands of literacy development represented in Figure 3.5: children's experiences of *reading* (environmental print as well as books and other texts), of *writing*, and of *oral language* (to include storytelling, phonological awareness and decontextualized talk).

For each strand of literacy, parents have the potential to provide opportunities, recognition, interaction, and a model (see Figure 3.6). Each cell in this matrix refers to an aspect of parental support for preschool literacy (e.g. providing a reading model, appropriate interaction in writing). It can be used to describe how particular families support children's literacy development but it is more useful to teachers as a *map of intervention possibilities*. One can ask of each cell in the matrix, 'What can school do to support the parent's role here?'

Finally, it helps to draw a distinction between the *focus* and the *location* of work with parents (see Figure 3.7). Although the focus may be on children's home learning, the work with parents to influence it could be located either in schools (or centres) or in the parents' homes. The branches in Figure 3.7 all represent possible forms of involvement in the teaching of literacy that need to be considered. It is important not to fall into the trap of thinking that parental involvement means getting parents into school to assist children's school learning — that is only one of four possibilities.

Figure 3.5:   Three strands of literacy experiences

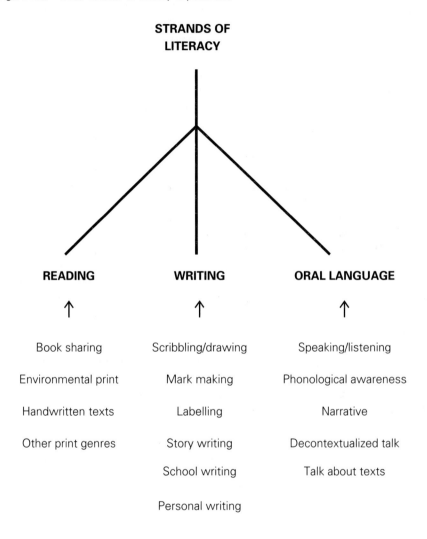

STRANDS OF LITERACY

READING	WRITING	ORAL LANGUAGE
↑	↑	↑
Book sharing	Scribbling/drawing	Speaking/listening
Environmental print	Mark making	Phonological awareness
Handwritten texts	Labelling	Narrative
Other print genres	Story writing	Decontextualized talk
	School writing	Talk about texts
	Personal writing	

The framework of ORIM (opportunities, recognition, interaction, model) in relation to different aspects of literacy development, and the concepts of focus and location, will be applied in the next chapter to work in the pre-school period, and in subsequent chapters to a range of work in the school years.

Figure 3.6: *A map of intervention possibilities*

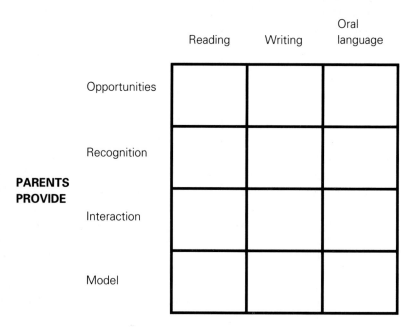

**STRANDS OF
LITERACY EXPERIENCE**

Figure 3.7: *Focus and location of work with parents*

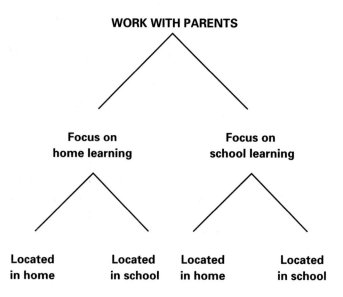

Chapter 4

Working with Parents of Preschool Children

If the learning of literacy in the print-rich cultures of industrialized countries begins well before school then so could the teaching of literacy, provided of course that it was fitted to children's developmental needs in that period. By 'teaching' I mean a deliberate activity intended to bring about someone else's learning. Much learning, of course, occurs without teaching. Teaching is not only carried out by professional teachers working in schools but also by pre-school teachers or other workers and, on occasions, by parents or other family members. Although some instances of teaching are clear it would be difficult to say exactly where the dividing line lies between deliberate teaching and other activities that promote learning. We need a better vocabulary to describe the many different ways in which people assist each other's learning. Meanwhile, the looseness of the term 'teaching' should not prevent us using it.

The teaching of literacy before school could be carried out either by parents or by preschool teachers or by both. If preschool teachers or other workers outside the family attempt it, the question they have to face is whether to involve parents in that teaching, and if so, how. The aims of this chapter are to assess to what extent at present there is preschool teaching of literacy, and to examine some ways of involving parents in that teaching.

The Place of Literacy in Preschool Education

Preschool teachers in Britain and many other countries have traditionally been reluctant to teach literacy. They have tended to resist pressures from parents and teachers of older children to 'start children off early' in reading and writing. In the past, some eradicated print from the nursery environment and emphasized alternatives to literacy — pictures not words, paint brushes not pens, pictures of animals, flowers or toys in place of children's names in the cloakroom.

One reason for this was a desire to protect the child from adult pressures, from requiring children to perform activities that they might find meaningless because they were not ready for them, and a desire to respect children's preschool life as valuable in itself, not just as a preparation for school life. There are deep-rooted feelings in the British nursery–infant tradition that can probably be traced back to the turn of the century. At that time under 5s enjoyed free access to full time schooling but decisions were taken to exclude them. One reason, amongst many, was probably that there was too much teaching of literacy, using inappropriate methods, at too early an age (Whitbread, 1972; Tizard *et al.*, 1976). Educators of the time were disturbed at the ways in which very young children were being taught reading and writing — seated for long periods, sometimes in galleries, in very large groups, subjected to techniques of mass instruction with a heavy reliance on rote learning, drill and practice, and with minimal opportunities for practical learning experiences. Nursery schooling, with different emphases, was advocated as a better way. In the years that followed, it never became widespread, but it kept alive child-centred practice in preschool education which today can provide a good context for developing literacy teaching.

Another reason for avoiding literacy could have been that nursery teachers were not much attracted to methods of teaching initial reading and writing in schools. There was the idea that children had to be taught distinct pre-reading skills. Walker (1975), for example, argued that 'success in the skills of reading depends on successful acquisition of the related subskills of prereading' (p.7) and 'in order to overcome the unique difficulties inherent in beginning reading it is necessary for the child to have *first* developed a minimum set of skills and capacities' (p.20, emphasis added). The skills in question were thought to be mainly perceptual (shape and letter discrimination, hand-eye coordination, left-right eye movements, visual memory, listening and auditory skills, phonemic discrimination, auditory memory, letter recognition, knowledge of letter names and sounds).

The idea that there were distinct pre-reading and pre-writing skills to be acquired before children could attempt the real thing, the tediousness of exercises to learn such skills, the use of reading schemes and flash cards, and the emphasis on writing as a manual skill all tended to deter preschool teachers from teaching literacy. Such methods would not have fitted in at all with the child-centred teaching style of most nursery teachers. As a result, the 'three Rs' were not a high priority for preschool teachers. In fact a very revealing Schools Council study found that in the early 1970s their aims mainly concerned *social* education (Taylor *et al.*, 1972). Preschool teachers in a large national sample drawn from nursery classes and schools were given a list of thirty possible educational objectives (compiled by researchers with the help of teacher discussion groups) and asked to rate the importance of each. The highest rated objective was helping children 'to get along with others and play cooperatively'. Interestingly, none of the thirty objectives explicitly mentioned reading or writing (or even preparation for these activities). The nearest was helping 'the child to develop a feeling for forms and styles of language, e.g. poetry' which ranked twenty-seventh out of the thirty for importance, just below helping 'the child acquire a positive attitude towards the skills and purposes of *eating*'.

The idea that preschool teachers should help children acquire positive attitudes to the skills and purposes of *reading* or *writing* as well as eating seems to have been overlooked at the time.

By the 1990s literacy had become a more explicit concern for many nursery teachers. As the emergent literacy perspective has become more widely appreciated many have begun to reorganize their classrooms so that literacy can emerge more easily, and be valued when it does. This trend is not confined to England (Dombey and Meek Spencer, 1994) but it is difficult to know how far this has gone.

A review of under-5s' education by HMI, based on some 300 visits and inspections of nursery and primary schools in England in the late 1980s (HMI, 1989), indicated a shift in what had become regarded as good practice. It acknowledged that preschool children are well used to seeing print in the environment, that many have an interest in reading, that some are already readers (although others need to learn the basics of using and enjoying books), and that children can record their ideas, experiences and feelings through writing as well as drawing and painting. Therefore, in relation to reading, the inspectors not only pointed out how teachers could foster preschool children's enjoyment of reading, but also how they could help them accurately relate meaning to the printed word and how they could begin to teach children about the relationship between letters and the initial sound of words in stories. In relation to writing, the inspectors pointed out how teachers could encourage children to write as part of their play activities by providing writing materials for them to record, initially in their own invented symbols, such things as shopping lists and telephone messages, how areas of the classroom can be set up as 'offices' or 'writing centres', how as children become eager to write, and their symbols closer to accepted letter forms, they can be taught to form letters and how teachers can write down for children what they say about their paintings, models or experiences. These recommendations were included among many others relating to the whole curriculum but they reflected, and legitimated, an increased emphasis on the teaching of literacy.

There has also been pressure in Britain in the 1990s to take preschool teaching of literacy more seriously as a result of the introduction of the national curriculum which specifies attainment targets and programmes of study for children from 5 years to 16. Although it would be wrong to allow the school curriculum entirely to shape preschool education, it is not unreasonable to expect preschool education to make a clear contribution to the task of schools (certainly, a refusal to do so would need considerable justification). There is also a need for continuity between preschool and school education. In relation to literacy (seen officially as part of the core subject of 'English') an examination of the original first level attainment targets listed in Table 4.1 shows that the contribution of preschool education can be very clear and direct. These attainment targets were intended to be appropriate for children aged 5 in their first year of compulsory schooling.

Three points should be noted about these attainment targets for reading,

Table 4.1: English national curriculum level 1 attainment targets

	STATEMENTS OF ATTAINMENT	
	Pupils should be able to	Example
READING	• recognize that print is used to carry meanings, in books and in other forms in the everyday world	*Point to and recognize own name; tell the teacher that a label on a container says what is inside or that the words in a book tell a story.*
	• begin to recognize individual words or letters in familiar contexts	*In role-play, read simple signs such as shop names or brand names; recognize 'bus-stop', 'exit', 'danger'.*
	• show signs of a developing interest in reading	*Pick up books and look at the pictures; choose books to hear or read.*
	• talk in simple terms about the content of stories, or information in non-fiction books	*Talk about characters and pictures, including likes and dislikes.*
WRITING	• use pictures, symbols or isolated letters, words or phrases to communicate meaning	*Show work to others, saying what writing and drawings mean.*
SPELLING	• begin to show an understanding of the difference between drawing and writing, and between numbers and letters	
	• write some letter shapes in response to speech sounds and letter names	*Initial letter of own name*
	• use at least single letters or groups of letters to represent whole words or parts of words	
HANDWRITING	• begin to form letters with some control over the size, shape and orientation of letters or lines of writing	

Source: DES, 1989.

writing and spelling. First, they assume a considerable amount of learning in the preschool years — either at home or in preschool education. Second, some preschool children will have reached those levels of development well before reaching school. Third, aiming for these attainment levels would be entirely consistent with an emergent literacy approach and what is rapidly being regarded as good practice in preschool education.

Teachers' Views about Preschool Literacy and Parents

If preschool teachers are beginning to see themselves as teachers of literacy too, are there any signs that they would like to involve parents in that teaching?

Research evidence is scarce but, as part of a study concerned with parents' and teachers' perspectives, some nursery class teachers were interviewed about preschool literacy (Hannon and James, 1990). Although the sample was small (ten teachers), it was drawn at random from a large LEA area, the interviewing was in-depth, and transcripts were analysed in detail. The study investigated teachers' views of the place of literacy in the preschool curriculum and what role, if any, they thought parents had in the teaching of literacy. The quotations that follow are from Hannon and James (1990).

The nursery teachers were aware of parents' interest in preschool literacy but they were worried about parents using inappropriate methods. For example, half the teachers felt parents concentrated too much on individual letters rather than whole words, both in reading and in writing.

> I tell them about letters — about not using the alphabet. Parents teach letters rather than whole words.

> They use capital letters, and some still teach the alphabet.

Several felt that parents would put too much pressure on children.

> No pressuring. They shouldn't be taught to read and write.

Several teachers seemed to believe that preschool education should be more concerned with general language development than literacy.

> If you haven't got language the words are meaningless. Nurseries are not for learning to read and write.

They suggested that parents should help children in the same way.

> I hope they take them out, introduce them to a wide variety of experiences, and encourage language to go along with that.

> Not to teach them reading but just to encourage them.

The general view of literacy in preschool education was expressed up by this teacher:

> There's no big rush to get them reading and writing. There's so much more they can do and it annoys me when parents say, 'When are you going to start learning them to read and write?' because there's so much more they can do — discovery learning and creative work, and getting confidence before they actually get a book.

In summary, the preschool teachers in this study did not see literacy as a central concern of the preschool curriculum (although various aspects of preparation for it may have been). Consequently, the idea of seriously involving parents in the teaching of literacy did not arise.

The Parents' Perspective

What do parents feel about their role in children's preschool literacy development? Several studies indicate the extent of parental involvement in children's preschool literacy. Hall *et al.* (1989) carried out a questionnaire survey of a large sample of parents and found many parents of preschool children doing something to help them learn to write. Studies of children who read early have found that they have had parents who have helped them in numerous ways from an early age (Durkin, 1966; Clark, 1976; Goelman *et al.*, 1984; Anbar, 1986). Naturalistic studies of disadvantaged, as well as other, preschool children indicate that some literacy tuition, however informal, is a part of family life (Heath, 1983; Taylor and Dorsey-Gaines, 1988).

In the Hannon and James study already referred to, there were forty parents of nursery children (a randomly selected sample from the classes of the teachers who were interviewed). Parents were interviewed at home about what literacy activities they were involved in with their children, what they and their children felt about them, and whether they had any uncertainties or need for advice.

It emerged that virtually all parents were taking a *very* active role in their children's literacy experiences. Activities ranged from reading shop signs, writing and reading greeting cards, watching television programmes, and looking together at papers, magazines and adults' books to book sharing and drawing/writing. Specific examples included the following:

We read him stories and tell him the letters.

If I write something I ask him what it is and tell him the letters and show him the words as we're reading.

We use the blackboard — put words on it.

We sit every night. She looks around the room and asks for the names of things to be written and copies them. I'm quite surprised at how well she does.

Many parents added — without prompting — that they did not want to put too much pressure on children.

I don't believe in pushing. I only do it if he asks. It's important to take it from the child's interest.

I don't sit down and say, 'let's learn'. It's based around fun.

It appeared in any case that most children needed no pressure to engage in literacy activity but found it enjoyable in itself.

> She pretends to read. She's not really reading — she just turns the pages and says the words.

> Books — loads of books. He loves books.

> She likes to write all sorts — shopping lists, stories, anything and everything.

Almost all the parents were confident that they had successfully taught their children some aspect of literacy and gave examples such as the following:

> Some of the letters of her name.

> That reading is interesting. He loves books. He'd sit all day just listening to stories. You've got to teach them to love books before they'll want to read.

> Written his name a lot — familiarized him with it. Got him interested in books — I take him to the library.

> Reading mostly. She understands what you read to her. Talks about books after — tells me what's happened.

Nevertheless, there was a widespread uncertainty amongst parents about whether they were helping in the right way. For example, a common problem in writing was whether to use upper case or lower case letters; in reading, whether to use letter names or try to refer to them by the sounds they make. This parent expressed a general feeling.

> A lot of parents don't do things with their kids because they don't want to do it wrong. If the way that you do it is different to what they do at school they're going to have to do it again. It would be best if they told us the right way before they started. When you come out of hospital if they just gave you a book about it because you're teaching them from being right little, aren't you, from being born really.

More than three-quarters of the parents said they would have liked advice but only one had ever asked a teacher. That may be because literacy did not figure much in the preschool education they saw in the nursery classes. When asked about the purpose of nursery activities, none of the parents mentioned reading or writing, and many seemed vague about why nurseries had the kinds of activities they did.

Stimulation in different things. We've not actually been told.

It learns them, doesn't it? Painting and that. Don't know about water. Why do they have water?

It is not surprising therefore that parents did not approach teachers for advice about how they could help with literacy.

I discuss it with other mums but never the teachers.

I wouldn't like them to feel that I was criticizing. You don't like to feel that you're telling somebody else how to do their job.

If they had asked for advice, it is likely (on the basis of the teacher comments quoted earlier) that they would have been advised *not to get involved at all* in many of the ways in which they were already involving themselves in children's literacy but to limit themselves to supporting spoken language and reading to children.

The general conclusion to be drawn from available research therefore is that parents of preschool children are active in promoting literacy development, would welcome the opportunity to be more fully involved in the teaching of literacy, but perceive (accurately) that teachers are uneasy about involving them.

Parental Involvement in Preschool Education

There is a strong tradition of parental involvement in preschool education that should encourage teachers to be more confident about work with parents focused on literacy. Some of clearest evidence of the benefits for children — in other aspects of preschool development — comes from intervention studies, particularly from the United States.

During the 1960s there were a number of well-designed experimental studies of preschool educational programmes in different parts of the US. The research concerned high quality programmes including preschool classes, with special curricula and varying forms of parental involvement. By 1974 it was possible for Urie Bronfenbrenner to review some of what had been learned. He concluded that where the intervention focused on children in group settings (nurseries, special centres, etc.) there were substantial intellectual gains in IQ in the first year but these could not be increased either by starting when children were younger or continuing for much longer than one year. When such programmes finished, the gains faded rather quickly, especially for children from the most deprived social and economic backgrounds. However, when the intervention also focused on the parent, results were much better. Substantial gains in IQ in the first year could be improved further by continuing the programme, and the younger the children started, the better. There also appeared to be benefits for siblings and for parents themselves. Bronfenbrenner summarized the findings thus.

> The evidence indicates that the involvement of the child's family as an active participant is critical to the success of any intervention program. Without such family involvement, any effects of intervention, at least in the cognitive sphere, appear to erode fairly rapidly once the program ends. In contrast, the involvement of the parents as partners in the enterprise provides an ongoing system which can reinforce the effects of the program while it is in operation, and help to sustain them after the program ends. (1974, p.55)

How were the parents involved in these programmes? The most common method was through home visiting, sometimes on its own, sometimes to complement work with children in a group setting. Visits by teachers might be for an hour or so weekly, or half an hour twice weekly. Some kind of structured curriculum for visits was followed and materials were usually introduced into the home for work with children. Direct parent participation in activities during the visit was encouraged but not always required. There was some evidence that the more successful forms of parent involvement were ones that deliberately sought to support parents in their role as educators and to avoid imposing visitors on them as 'experts'. In addition to visits some programmes also had meetings in school and informal contact between the workers and parents.

Later there was a follow-up study by the Consortium for Longitudinal Studies of children from eleven well-designed preschool intervention experiments in the US (Lazar *et al.*, 1982) which found several benefits years afterwards in terms of reduced likelihood of special education placement or being held back a grade in school, high school graduation, employment, take-up of post-school education, and other social outcomes. The findings also indicated that the more parental involvement (home visits by teachers, direct educational involvement, services for parents as well as children) in the programme, the more positive were the outcomes.

In Britain, research into preschool intervention has been much more modest. However, it seems that studies of programmes that have involved parents, usually through home visiting (e.g. the West Riding EPA Project reported in Smith, 1975) may have influenced practitioners more than those which concentrated exclusively on work with children in group settings (e.g. an NFER experiment reported by Woodhead, 1976). There has been a continuing interest in the potential of home visiting to assist young children's education by involving their parents (Hirst and Hannon, 1990).

To summarize, there is clear evidence that parents can be involved in the preschool years and their involvement can be of considerable educational benefit. If it works for other areas of development, why not for literacy too?

School-focused Involvement

In the last chapter a distinction was drawn between parental involvement focused on school learning and that focused on home learning (see Figure 3.8). Both kinds are possible at the preschool level, and the work with parents to achieve it can either be located in homes or in centres such as preschools. Let us begin with the most obvious form of involvement — involving parents in children's school learning and working with them in the school setting to achieve this. What can be done to involve parents in children's literacy learning in the preschool? Everything depends on how the nursery or reception teacher organizes the classroom environment — whether to foster the emergence of literacy or to smother it. Assuming the former, activities that parents could undertake with children include the following:

- sharing books;
- cutting/sticking, using captions;
- making books;
- helping at drawing/writing tables;
- providing a model of writing or reading;
- adding to classroom print displays;
- writing or reading with a computer;
- supporting literacy-related sociodramatic play;
- teaching nursery rhymes;
- identifying/collecting logos and signs.

Note that parents could be engaged in these activities with their own children or other parents' children, or both.

The teacher–parent interaction to make this form of involvement happen would probably be based in the classroom, 'on the job' as it were, or elsewhere within the school, that is, the right-hand branch of Figure 3.7. It could take place at home (i.e. the adjacent branch) but it is doubtful whether it would be an efficient or justifiable use of teacher time to make home visits to sustain school-focused involvement. The point is that there has to be some teacher–parent interaction located somewhere if parents are to understand the point of what they do in school, especially in relation to literacy where there is scope for misunderstandings between parents and teachers about the rationale for it in the nursery and the most helpful role for adults to take in promoting it.

There are some disadvantages with school-located school-focused parent involvement. Not all parents can come into a school or centre for perfectly understandable reasons related to work or domestic commitments to other children or dependent family members. Some parents, therefore, through no lack of interest in their children, are bound to be excluded. Also, there can sometimes be practical difficulties if parents work with other people's children. Should all parents be encouraged to take such a role in school, even under the supervision of a teacher? Other parents may object, and some teachers will be uneasy about too open an invitation to parents to help in school. Finally, having parents in school is not really playing to their strengths which are in the home with their own children. For some parents (those perhaps with unhappy memories of their own schooling), the school may even be alien territory. Involvement should aim to build on parents' strengths rather than their weaknesses, and to that extent this kind of involvement has its limitations.

Home-focused Involvement

Home-focused involvement does not suffer from the same disadvantages. It means playing to parents' strengths and, in principle, all parents can be involved. It does present a challenge, however. How can teachers influence the subtleties of parent–child interaction in the home in an area such as literacy? Do parents welcome their attempts to do so? Are home literacy practices affected? And, most important of all, what difference, if any, does it make to children's literacy development? There have been some studies of home-focused preschool parental involvement programmes in literacy that begin to answer to these questions.

In a British study reported by Swinson (1985) parents of preschool children (aged 3 to 4 years) were encouraged to read to their children from books made available from a school. There were two initial meetings for parents to discuss home reading to children and to provide general advice on 'good practice'. The project ran for most of a school year during which the level of daily home reading rose close to 100 per cent (from a previous level of around 15 per cent). At the end there were gains in oral vocabulary and verbal comprehension, and, in a follow-up after school entry, gains on word matching and letter identification, compared to children in a control group. In the Calderdale Pre-School Parent Book Project in England, parents of nursery children were systematically encouraged to borrow books from project schools (Griffiths and Edmonds, 1986). The focus of involvement was the home learning experiences of children but the teacher–parent interaction (mainly meetings) was located in school. Take-up over an eight-month period was high, parents and teachers viewed the project positively, and there were some gains in measures of children's literacy development. Wade (1984) has reported an experiment in which there was an attempt to enhance young children's story-telling ability. It included some preschool children and involved parents at home.

In the United States, McCormick and Mason (1986) have reported a programme in which children had 'little books' mailed to them in the months before they started kindergarten. Despite minimal parent–teacher interaction there was evidence that this modest intervention had some impact on literacy attainment at the end of the kindergarten year. The Pittsburgh Beginning with Books Project has provided packs of books for much younger children, without parent–teacher interaction, and on a very much larger scale with thousands of children (Locke, 1988; Segel and Friedberg, 1991). There has since been a similar but smaller scale initiative in Britain (Wade and Moore, 1993). Lujan, *et al.* (1986) have described a programme of school-based workshops for parents of preschool children. Edwards (1989) studied ways of changing parents' interaction with preschool children during shared storybook reading. A rare attempt to influence children's writing development has been reported by Green (1987) who describes a project in which parents of kindergarten children were shown three ways to help them at home (by acting as a scribe, by writing to children, and by encouraging children to write themselves). There was a positive response from parents and measurable literacy gains for the children in comparison with a control group. All of these interventions have been consistent with an emergent literacy orientation and, although often located in schools or centres they have all been home-focused. A report by Winter and Rouse (1990) has described a programme with a more explicit emergent literacy orientation which, because it involved parents through home visiting, was home-located as well as home-focused.

In Table 4.2 there is an attempt to identify what these initiatives were trying to change in terms of the ORIM framework discussed in the previous chapter (see Figure 3.6). It can be seen that most studies have concentrated on reading (usually of books) and most have sought to increase *opportunities*. There has been less work on environmental print and writing. There have been some attempts to change parents' *interaction* with children but very little explicit concern with their *recognition* of preschool literacy achievements or how they provide a *model* of literacy. A project in Sheffield, England attempted to fill in some of the gaps.

The Sheffield Early Literacy Development Project

The Sheffield Early Literacy Development Project set out to find practical ways of working with parents to promote preschool literacy development in the home (Hannon *et al.*, 1991). Designed principally as a feasibility study, incorporating a qualitative evaluation, it did not attempt directly to measure the effects of such work on children's literacy development.

The project developed methods of work with parents — home-focused but located in both home and school — targeted primarily on children in the middle of the preschool period — around 2.5 to 3 years of age — but suitable for other preschool children in a family too. The focus for the work is shown by the ticked cells in Table 4.3. The focus on reading emphasized children's experiences of environmental print as much as books. There was little direct attempt to influence the oral language strand.

Families were invited to take part in the project solely on the basis of living close to the project school and having children in the target age range. As an exploratory study, it had to have a small enough sample to permit

Table 4.2: Research into home-focused preschool literacy intervention involving parents

Research report	STRANDS OF LITERACY			ASPECTS OF PARENT'S ROLE INFLUENCED			
	Reading*	Writing	Oral language	Opportunities	Recognition	Interaction	Model
Wade (1984)	✓		✓	✓		✓	✓
Swinson (1985)	✓			✓		✓	
McCormick and Mason (1986)	✓			✓			
Griffiths and Edmonds (1986)	✓			✓			
Lujan et al. (1986)	✓	✓		✓	✓	✓	?
Green (1987)	✓	✓		✓	✓	✓	✓
Edwards (1989)	✓			✓	✓	✓	
Winter and Rouse (1990)	✓	?		✓	✓	?	
Segel and Friedberg (1991)	✓			✓			
Hannon et al. (1991)	✓	✓		✓	✓	✓	✓

Note: *'Reading' confined to books except in Hannon et al. (1991) which focused on environmental print too.

Table 4.3: Aspects of children's early literacy and the parent's role explored in the Sheffield Early Literacy Development Project

STANDS OF PRESCHOOL
LITERACY EXPERIENCE

		Reading*	Writing	Oral language
	Opportunities	✔	✔	
	Recognition	✔	✔	
PARENTS PROVIDE	Interaction	✔	✔	✔
	Model	✔	✔	

Note: *'Reading' included environmental print as well as books.
Source: Hannon *et al.*, 1991

detailed case studies (twenty children, from fourteen families). Many of the families were disadvantaged. Several parents admitted to difficulties themselves in reading or writing but all children had English as a first language.

Three main methods of work with parents were devised: provision of literacy materials, home visiting and meetings. These are outlined below but fuller details have been provided by Weinberger *et al.* (1990).

Provision of literacy materials
Books for children and parents were made available to borrow for use at home. There was also a booklclub where similar books could be purchased. Other materials provided were intended to encourage recognition of environmental print and the development of writing and included magazines and catalogues, forms, cards and envelopes, plain paper, lined paper, pencil, sharpener and ballpoint pen. The literacy materials (in addition to whatever was already in the home) were introduced through a home visit.

Home visits
Some families had a series of six fortnightly home visits from one of the researchers. In planning these an attempt was made to strike a balance between the need for a flexible child-centred approach and the need for coherent coverage of key aspects of early literacy development. Visits were planned on the basis of a 'review–input–plan' structure. Each child's literacy activities

since the previous visit were *reviewed* with the parent. A new idea or activity was *introduced*, building on the child's previous experiences. A *plan* of what might be done next with the child was agreed with the parent. (This series of visits followed the initial visit at which programme materials were introduced into the home.) Further books for borrowing and replacement drawing/writing materials were brought by the visitor. Other activities included making books, using photographs, cutting, sticking and labelling, finding print in the home and neighbourhood, matching logos, and trying different kinds of drawing/writing materials. Children's work saved by parents was reviewed to show development (between visits and over longer periods of time).

Meetings

A series of five meetings was held for parents to give them an opportunity to share experiences in a small group and to have a more formal input from the research team. A crèche was available when necessary. Topics included family literacy, print in the environment, the development of writing from early mark making, how children enjoy books, judging quality in books, sharing books and stories with children, using public libraries, methods of literacy teaching in schools, recognizing and recording aspects of literacy development. Methods used were group discussion, videos, slides, overhead projector transparencies of children's writing, displays of books, handouts, information about research, sharing of observations, and a 'jigsaw' profile of literacy development. Handouts were prepared after each meeting summarizing information given and parents' views. Meetings took place in the school except for a group visit to the local library at which all children were enrolled as library members. Books for borrowing and additional drawing/writing materials were made available at the meetings (which followed the initial visit to introduce programme materials into the home).

One method of assisting parents' *recognition* of preschool literacy development was to use a 'jigsaw' in which the various pieces showed examples of children's early achievements in reading and writing — achievements that many parents might not have recognized as such. Figure 4.1 shows a development of this idea. The jigsaw was printed on a sheet of paper and parents were invited to shade in pieces according to whether they had observed their children doing these things. The metaphor of the jigsaw is helpful in conveying the idea that literacy has many different 'pieces' but they do not have to be fitted together in any definite order to make a whole. In the version in Figure 4.2 the idea has been developed further by not having a rectangular boundary to the jigsaw and by having blanks for parents to fill in according to what *they* think are significant achievements, thus suggesting that literacy is not bounded and that parents' views about what it consists of are important too.

The overall findings from the Sheffield Project reported by Hannon *et al.* (1991), based on a range of data (field notes, samples of children's work,

Figure 4.1: *A way of helping parents recognize children's preschool literacy development. Part of a jigsaw that parents are invited to shade in to show what their children can do (blank pieces for them to write in achievements they consider significant)*

Source: Derived from Weinberger *et al.*, 1990, p.23.

records of book borrowing, observations and pre-programme and post-programme interviews), indicated that take-up and participation levels were high, there was no dropout, the intervention was welcomed by parents, and both they and the project team experienced it as meaningful. The impact on parent–child interaction in the home was assessed in terms of how some strands of literacy experience (environmental print, early writing and sharing books) were changed by some aspects of the parent's role (providing a model, opportunities and recognition) represented in Figure 4.1. It was possible to identify changes in each of the cells in that figure although in some areas (e.g. parents providing opportunities for book sharing) the impact was more striking than in others (e.g. parents providing a model for using environmental print). There was some evidence that home-based methods had more impact than school-based ones, particularly in book sharing.

Implications for Practice, Policy and Research

There is then obviously considerable potential for involving parents in the preschool teaching of literacy. A limiting factor is the reluctance of some pre-school teachers to accept literacy as a major concern of preschool education but it is likely that increasing numbers of them will see that, from an emergent literacy perspective, a concern with literacy means extending the tradition of child-centred nursery teaching rather than compromising it.

The ORIM framework can aid the development of practice. Work with parents can be structured in terms of helping the emergence of children's literacy through experience of environmental print, book sharing, writing and oral language, and helping parents appreciate what they can provide in respect of each of these. It is also necessary to be clear about the focus and location of work with parents. Research has also shown that parents respond well to efforts to involve them, that there is a range of feasible methods, and that there are encouraging indications that these have an impact on children's literacy experiences before school entry. This should be sufficient to encourage preschool teachers to try some of the methods described in this chapter with some confidence that they are feasible and worthwhile. All this is not quite enough however. There is clearly a need for further research in at least four areas.

First, the framework of *opportunities–recognition–interaction–model* and *reading/writing/oral language* suggests a research agenda. In future studies, techniques need to be developed to explore all aspects of the parent's role, and to detect changes when they occur.

Second, there is an underlying issue that needs to be more thoroughly explored. In what ways are the conditions for the emergence of children's literacy any less favourable in disadvantaged families? Emergent literacy research has emphasized what *all* children know about reading and writing in the early years, rather than what some may *not* know. The same research tradition has stressed the parallels between the development of written language and the development of spoken language (where, in the past, 'common sense' assumptions about 'deficits' have been so misleading). On the other hand, what the Sheffield study found about pre-existing family literacy activity suggests that there is significant variation in children's experiences. It would be helpful to have more research comparing specific aspects of preschool literacy experience across a range of family backgrounds. Research in this area has to be sensitive to some fundamental theoretical difficulties in distinguishing between children who have 'less' literacy and those whose literacy is simply different from 'school literacy'. Practice has to be sensitive to the question of whether one is extending family literacy or imposing school literacy.

Third, there need to be more experimental studies. The Sheffield project, for example, adopted a non-experimental design that was appropriate for determining the feasibility of intervention and for exploring the probable impact on children's and parents' experiences but it does not tell us what the impact has been on the children's literacy development itself. Yet this is something we need to know if we are to decide whether this kind of intervention justifies the costs incurred. An experimental study should measure costs as well as benefits, and would have to overcome problems of measuring literacy development in the preschool period, at school entry, and later.

Fourth, there are other methods of work to be developed and evaluated. For example, there is evidence — both survey and experimental — that the development of phonological awareness in the preschool period aids progress in early reading (Bryant and Bradley, 1985; Maclean *et al.*, 1987; Goswami and Bryant, 1990). There is obvious potential for sharing this information with parents and developing parent–child activities involving letters, sounds and rhymes that may be both enjoyable in themselves as well as helpful for children's literacy development. There are other aspects of oral language, highlighted by the work of other investigators, which could be the basis of work with parents, for example, storytelling (Wells, 1987) or decontextualized talk (Snow, 1991).

The main policy issues to be faced concern resources, training and future research. It certainly requires resources (such as staff time, some materials and use of buildings) in order to make an impact. If policy makers try to increase work with parents without allocating resources, it is unlikely to happen. This is particularly so if home-located methods such as home visiting are employed. Training for this kind of work with parents is slowly being acknowledged as a problem. Preschool teachers are poorly prepared in their initial training for work with parents. Whether there will be any future development and research in this area in the future is also a matter of policy. There need to be decisions at a national level that such a programme of research is necessary and about what priorities it should address.

This chapter has concerned parent involvement before school but it will become clear in the next chapter that many of the ideas continue to apply to what happens after children start school.

Chapter 5

Working with Parents of School-age Children

In Chapter 2 we saw that one of the main strategies to involve parents in the teaching of literacy for school-age children has been encouraging and supporting parents in hearing reading at home. In this chapter I examine the importance of this form of involvement and look at the practical implications for schools wanting to implement it. By concentrating on this particular form of involvement I hope to illuminate issues that apply to many others too.

The phrase 'hearing a child read' (or 'listening to a child read') covers activities that go far beyond merely attending to what children say aloud. It includes a whole range of moves that might encourage or assist children when they encounter difficulties reading (and also when they do not). Unfortunately there is no convenient term or phrase that readily conveys these possibilities. In North America there is the phrase 'guided oral reading' but, apart from its unfamiliarity in the British context, it implies a more directive role for the hearer than may often be the case. Teachers in the early school years have generally taken the view that hearing young children read is an important activity, full of teaching possibilities. From this point of view encouraging parents to do it too is a very significant form of involvement. But one could take a different view. It might be regarded as so simple and ordinary as to be marginal to children's reading development. One writer, for example, has dismissed it, in comparison to other forms of involvement, as 'often a lightweight intervention' (Topping, 1985). Therefore it is desirable to try to get some sense of its importance, and of whether it is worth implementing, before considering practical questions.

Let us look at the issue in terms of the framework introduced in Chapter 3 that suggested what children need to acquire literacy. In terms of *opportunities* children obviously need appropriate reading materials. By 'appropriate' we require, at the very least, that the materials are correctly written in the child's language. It helps if the materials are also appropriate in terms of not being too difficult initially, and if they appeal to young children's interests. Nowadays there are many excellent illustrated books, not usually to be found in structured reading schemes, which are highly appropriate in this sense (Bennett, 1983). However, one should not be too prescriptive about what counts as 'appropriate'. Newspapers, cornflake packets, advertisements, road signs, and even flash cards can be appropriate in some circumstances. In the past, some children probably learned to read using difficult adult material such as the Bible. Children's own writing or sentence-making produced under guidance can also highly appropriate.

A second key requirement is for *appropriate interaction* when the child actually attempts to read (aloud). He or she then needs someone to provide feedback and assistance. All learning requires feedback and in the case of learning to read the feedback often involves telling the learner whether something has been read accurately or not. It might also involve encouragement to read for meaning. Further assistance includes providing words or phrases that the child cannot read, and giving general encouragement. Encouragement depends upon whoever provides it being able to *recognize* reading achievement from the earliest steps, to using different strategies to puzzle out new words in a book, to responding critically to all sorts of texts. Finally, during a shared reading episode the adult may read to the child, thereby not only sharing the task but also providing a reading *model*. All these are activities that fall under the umbrella phrase 'hearing reading'.

We have here a useful list that allows us to assess the value of a form of parental involvement in the teaching of reading that simply consists of encouraging parents to hear children read books provided by school. Specifically, we can assess the potential contributions of teachers and parents.

Take the requirement for appropriate interaction. Although good teachers can certainly stimulate children's literary excitement and their desire to learn to read, they are at a disadvantage compared to parents. Not only do parents have a deeper, more powerful, relationship with their own children than teachers can aspire to, but parents are better placed to exploit those moments in the day, from waking to bedtime, when children's desire to read is at its strongest and when they find the activity most meaningful. In comparison, classroom learning experiences are all too often artificial, hurried and unexciting for children. Therefore any form of parental involvement that makes use of parents' power to motivate makes sense.

A child's teacher can provide feedback and assistance, but only to a limited extent. Class teachers are under tremendous time pressures; they have to relate continuously to large numbers of children, and they have to deal with many interruptions. At best, most class teachers can only devote a few minutes, three or four days a week, to hearing a child read. Parents, on the other hand, can obviously give far more time and, with their closer relationship with the child and opportunities for quiet, they are in a position to provide valuable help. There might be some question about how the quality of parents' help compares to that provided by teachers (we shall look at some research into this question in the next chapter) but, on the face of it, involving parents in this role makes sense. Also, as we saw earlier a great many parents already try to help their children by hearing them read and there is a case for schools supporting them in this rather then ignoring their efforts.

Now take the requirement for appropriate learning materials. Here it is teachers who have an advantage over parents. By virtue of their training, experience, and familiarity with what is published they ought to know a great deal about reading materials for young children. They should also be able to provide a wider range of appropriate books from classroom and school libraries than most parents could afford to provide from their own resources. Therefore any form of parental involvement in which teachers take responsibility for providing the reading materials (or the range from which choices can be made) makes sense. This is likely to be a considerable help to poorer parents whose children may have very few, if any, suitable books at home. In their survey of middle-class and working-class children at the age of 7, John and Elizabeth Newson (1977) found what they described as a 'massive class difference' in book ownership. Another study by Liz Whitehurst of middle-class children found some 7-year-olds with book collections running into hundreds (Whitehurst, 1983). At the other extreme, in the course of another study (Hannon, 1987), it became clear to me that many children from poor working-class families have virtually no suitable reading materials at home. Obviously, sending school reading books home in such circumstances could have a considerable impact on children's opportunities to learn to read.

To summarize, an analysis of what is involved in learning to read reveals basic requirements that could best be met by teachers and parents *in combination*. There are good grounds for seeing the simple and entirely straightforward strategy of encouraging parents to hear children read books provided by the school as an important form of involvement, well worth closer consideration.

School-focused or home-focused?

One way in which parents have been involved in the teaching of reading for some years is by coming into school and hearing children read in class under the general supervision of a teacher. This is school-focused involvement. Parents may take the initiative in offering to help but, typically, a class teacher or a headteacher invites parents to help in school. There may be an open invitation to all parents or a specific invitation to parents selected either for what they can offer or for what they are thought to need. Sometimes a general invitation is issued but it is found that parents only respond when approached individually. Parents may be asked to come in for a short period of time during one or more days during the week. Once in the classroom they are likely to hear a small number of children read, usually a group of the better readers.

Hearing children read may be regarded as one end of a continuum of school-focused involvement. At the other end are to be found less direct forms of involvement such as helping in a school library (covering books etc.) or helping on school visits and outings. The NFER survey carried out in 1977 by Cyster *et al.* (1980) found that parents were hearing children read under the supervision of teachers in about one-quarter of primary schools (the less direct forms of involvement were generally more common). A later survey, by Barry Stierer (1985), suggested that by 1984 this form of involvement had increased for he found that 45 per cent of primary schools had parents helping with children's reading in school and the involvement in virtually all cases included hearing children read.

It is easy to see that there can be benefits from having parents hear children read in school. For children there are increased opportunities to enjoy the invaluable experience of reading to someone. For parents there is the chance for genuine direct involvement in children's education, ease of entry into their child's school, and a legitimate role once inside. For teachers there is help in a part of their teaching that is time-consuming and in which they can rarely be satisfied that they have done enough. With the help of parents they can be freed to concentrate their skills on those children in the class who need them most (often, according to Stierer's study, the younger or poorer readers).

Yet there are drawbacks that seriously restrict the practical value of this and other forms of school-based involvement. A basic issue is whether the parents come into school to work with their own children or with those of other parents. If parents just hear their own children read to them this has benefits only for those children whose parents are able to come into school (and benefits only for those parents able to come in). Parents who go out to work during the day and those whose domestic responsibilities (regarding, for example, babies or invalid relatives) make it very difficult to find time to spend in school are automatically excluded. Fathers who are in employment are particularly likely to be excluded (so that the parents who come in to school tend to be mothers and the all-female ethos of early childhood education is reinforced). What are the excluded parents likely to feel as a result? More to the point, how do children feel if they see their classmates enjoying their parents' presence in school when they cannot?

Are matters improved if parents come in to work with several children? Not necessarily, for it is still only some children's parents who are involved although it must be said that more children — perhaps all — could receive extra attention. The major drawback here is that one is no longer dealing with the involvement of parents so much as the involvement of what Stierer terms 'reading volunteers'. The involvement no longer exploits the quality of a child's relationship with his or her parent; it might as well be any adult helping. Three problems follow. First, there is the question of the adult's suitability. Schools might not be prepared to let just anyone help in such a delicate activity but that means selecting 'suitable' parents and being prepared to turn some away. Even if this problem can be overcome, a second one remains. Some parents might not agree with the school that certain reading volunteers are suitable for 'helping' their children. They send their children to school to be taught by teachers, not by neighbours whom they may not trust, either for what they do in school or what they do out of it. Such objections are indeed encountered in practice. The third problem is a more general one concerning the function of 'volunteers' (usually women, and unpaid) in schools in a climate of cuts in education. Will this development mask a shortage of properly trained and paid teachers? Is it a consequence of it? There is undoubtedly a case to be made for greater community involvement in schools and it would be wrong to suggest that everyone contributing to the work of schools has to be paid for it. Nonetheless, this problem, especially in conjunction with the others, should make schools uneasy about too readily promoting the use of volunteers.

These practical limitations are not fatal to this form of school-based parental involvement. There should be no question of preventing parents coming in to hear their own children read; indeed, they should be welcomed. The point is that, in practice, this cannot be relied upon as a principal strategy for involving *all* parents in the teaching of reading.

Many of the problems disappear if we stop thinking about parental involvement as a matter of 'bringing parents into school'. As we saw earlier, the case for parental involvement is strongest in relation to what parents can do, or are already trying to do, *in the home*. Parents can be encouraged to hear their children read at home, and schools can provide the appropriate materials by sending school books home with children (home-focused involvement). No parents need be automatically excluded from this, and it is parents being involved with their own children rather than with other people's children. To explore the practicalities of this form of involvement, let us consider how it works in a typical school.

Implementing a Reading at Home Scheme

How someone implements or increases parental involvement in a school depends very much on who they are. Headteachers, teachers and outsiders each have their particular strengths and weaknesses, related to their roles, in making changes in a school's practice.

The class teacher's role is decisive. Without his or her commitment there can be very little genuine parental involvement. Those seeking to change things from outside the classroom — be they headteachers, specialist teachers, advisers, educational psychologists, governors, or parents — all have to reckon with the fact that it is the class teacher who, through daily contact with children and parents, determines whether involvement is experienced by those concerned as exciting and purposeful or as a tedious charade. However, class teachers are not all-powerful. They can impede other people's attempts to increase parental involvement but if they wish to move in that direction themselves they can encounter difficulties. Some headteachers are still hostile to the idea of allowing school reading books to go home and encouraging parents to hear children read. It is not unknown in such circumstances for class teachers to involve parents surreptitiously but this requires considerable self-confidence and perhaps some incompetence on the part of the head. A class teacher might also have to face hostility from colleagues or indifference from a headteacher in which case a measure of self-confidence is still needed. Obviously, the most favourable circumstances for innovation occur when the initiative for involving parents comes from a class teacher who has the active support of the headteacher and colleagues. Therefore for a class teacher wanting to introduce this form of parental involvement, the first step should be to identify and, if possible, increase whatever support may be available within the school.

If the initiative comes from a headteacher then he or she has to convince teachers that what is proposed is both desirable and feasible. This cannot be achieved by a simple directive from the top but how it is done will depend upon the leadership style of the head. In some schools the climate in terms of attitudes to parents, staff relationships and receptivity to innovation will be favourable. If teachers are not already convinced of the value of working with parents and if they are not generally open-minded about developing their practice then very careful thought needs to be given to preparing them for a new role. The deeper their doubts, the more time it is worth devoting to exploring their views as well as the case for involvement. It might be worth extending ordinary staff discussions into some kind of school-focused in-service training (Long, 1986). Heads as initiators also have some responsibility for weighing the need to develop parental involvement against other priorities for the school. This becomes particularly important if there is a question of resources such as staff time or money being switched from one area to another (e.g. from small-group remedial teaching to home visiting).

Outsiders (that is, those who are not members of the teaching staff of a school) have the greatest difficulties in initiating change. In some cases they may be called in as 'experts' of one kind or another. This role has sometimes been played by educational psychologists or by in-service trainers of one kind or another. Others, such as school governors or parents, may be regarded as 'low status' in that they do not usually possess professional credibility. Some schools may take their suggestions for increased parental involvement seriously but others will be inclined to take them merely as an invitation to 'explain' their current practice. Outside contributions can sometimes be welcomed by self-confident and truly professional teachers in which case they can produce considerable changes. Elsewhere much depends upon outsiders' skills in working with groups of adults, in this case principally groups of teachers contemplating change. Staff need to feel they own any scheme that is introduced so the outsiders have to know when to withdraw and, if a scheme is successful, they have to be prepared for the possibility that their role as initiators will be forgotten.

Some Practical Questions

Whoever decides to implement a reading at home scheme — whether they are working alone or with others in a school — needs some kind of plan. If there has previously been very little involvement, it is unwise to try to involve all children and all parents in a school overnight. Even a class teacher working alone ought to think twice about suddenly working with parents of all children in the class. A step by step approach allows teachers to accustom themselves gradually to a new practice and difficulties can be ironed out before they grow too large.

This implies a selection, at least initially, of some children out of all those who could be included. There might in any case be a desire for selective involvement in order, for example, to help failing readers. However, practical considerations suggest that this is unwise. The problem is that it will soon be apparent, both to children and to parents, why certain children are taking their reading books home. Parental involvement will be seen as something just for children who are 'behind' rather than a good for all. The children (and the parents) concerned are likely to feel stigmatized and resentful about participating at all. Consequently, in the long run, this sort of selective involvement may well be counter-productive as well as unfair to the excluded children and their parents. Nevertheless, in the short run, there may still be a need for some sort of selection. One solution is to select a number of children entirely at random explaining clearly to all concerned why this is being done. This may strike some parents as an odd procedure so an alternative might be to select children according to age. Within a school it could be decided for example to start a scheme with the year 1 or year 2 (Kindergarten or Grade 1) children. Within a class it could be just the summer-born children or all children above or below a given age. Such criteria are likely to be generally accepted and they can easily be widened as time goes on so that ultimately all children are included.

Hearing children read is really only an appropriate way of helping them during a certain period in their reading development. For very young children who cannot read at all it is obviously inapplicable. For older children who can read fluently and silently there is the danger that they will find reading aloud a frustrating experience that will inhibit the development of further reading skills. Which age groups in a school should be included? Most reported schemes have focused on children aged 5 to 8. Chronological age can only be a rough guide as this three-year target age range covers an enormous range of reading ages. Some of the youngest children will be able to read better than some of the oldest, and there will be children with chronological ages above and below the range who will have reading ages within it. Also, the variation from one school to another, depending on catchment areas, can be enormous. A flexible approach is called for. Classes or year groups in which the majority of children are at a stage to benefit from reading aloud to someone can be included in a scheme but some modifications will be necessary for the minority. For instance, parents of younger children might be advised to read stories to their children or to talk about picture books with them. Parents of older children needing to extend their skills might be encouraged to concentrate on discussing their children's reading with them. In both instances these children take school books home like all their classmates but what their parents do at home is different.

There are some other details of a reading at home scheme that have to be settled at the outset. How often should children take books home? The choice here probably lies between aiming for two or three times a week and aiming for every night. Both have been tried and found to be practicable. Two or three times a week will seem a reasonable frequency to many people but doing something every weekday has the advantage of being an unvarying routine that is less easily forgotten.

Another issue that sometimes causes problems concerns which books children should take home. Some schools distinguish between children's 'reading books' and other books that children have in school. The 'reading book' from which children are supposed to learn to read is likely to be chosen by the teacher, it may be taken from a structured reading scheme, and it is the one that a child reads to his or her teacher. The 'other book' (sometimes it may be called the 'library book') is likely to be chosen by the child from the classroom or school library for private reading and enjoyment. Some teachers are happy for the 'other book' to go home but not the 'reading book'. The distinction between the two sorts of reading matter is, to say the least, highly questionable, in so far as it assumes that learning and enjoyment can and should be separated. However, if parents are to be seriously involved in the teaching of reading there should be no question of providing them with less appropriate materials than those used by teachers. It is the 'reading book' that should go home. One reading scheme published in Britain has a separate range of school books for parents to use at home. A brochure from the publishers describes this as a 'big step forward in the teacher–parent partnership' but it seems more like an attempt to disguise parental exclusion.

This takes us to the question of how the idea of involvement should be presented to parents and what advice should be given to them. Schools with a tradition of good home–school relations, and even those where school reading books have been allowed home, need to think about this as carefully as those for whom a reading at home scheme is a more radical departure. It is vital that all parents are told clearly and in advance that their children will be coming home with books and what they are being asked to do. Imagine the uncertainty that even the most confident and willing parent might feel if their 5-year-old was to arrive home without warning with a book which he or she must read to the parent. How much should be read? Suppose the child does not want to read? What to do when the child has difficulties? What is it all for anyway? There are several methods of communication that can be used to ease these problems — letters sent home, chance encounters with parents in school, individual or group meetings in school, home visiting — but what really matters here is what should be communicated rather than the means used. It should be made clear that the school is inviting, not in any way requiring, parents to join a scheme. Parents must not feel that they are being asked to take on a heavy and never-ending commitment. Instead they could be told, for

Table 5.1: Some dos and don'ts suggested to parents in the Belfield Reading Project

- Do make sure that the atmosphere is happy and relaxed.
- Do let the child sit very close to you.
- Do talk to the child about the picture first.
- Do read the page to the child first.
- Do place just a slight emphasis on new words and point to them at the same time.
- Do give the child plenty of time to read to you.
- Do smooth out difficulties by telling the child words he or she does not know. Repeat the whole sentence that the word is in and then let the child do it again.
- Do go back to the picture again and discuss whatever is relevant to the reading.
- Do give the child plenty of praise for effort.

- Don't make reading an unpleasant task.
- Don't threaten to tell the teacher if the child does not read.
- Don't make the child think that he or she is in competition with anyone else.
- Don't show anxiety about lack of interest.
- Don't be afraid to ask for help and advice from any of the teachers however trivial you feel the trouble is.
- Don't have the 'telly' on.

Source: Jackson and Hannon, 1981

example, that they are being asked to spend just five to ten minutes hearing their child read on so many evenings a week for, say, just one term in the first instance. The probable benefits to the child and the parent's advantages as an educator should be stressed. Any procedures such as the use of reading cards detailing suggested reading need to be explained too.

What advice should be given about how to hear children read? Teachers may hold different views about this but the points in Table 5.1, from a guide written by Beryl Page and used in the Belfield Reading Project, might be considered (Jackson and Hannon, 1981). It was intended for young children just beginning reading but many of the points are relevant to older children too.

The idea must also be explained to children. Time should be taken in class to explain why they are taking books home and what they are supposed to do with them. Their enthusiasm and pride in what they are doing should be nurtured for it will reward the parents and teachers participating.in a scheme and make it more likely to succeed. Teachers can devise classroom routines (e.g. for collecting books at home time, bags or plastic wallets for carrying them) that can make it easy and fun for children to play their part.

If parental involvement in the teaching of reading is to be taken as seriously as other aspects of the curriculum then record keeping ought to be taken as seriously here as elsewhere. What is required is nothing elaborate or time-consuming but a simple system for noting what books children take home, whether parents do hear reading, and what difficulties or successes are experienced. One solution is to have reading cards to accompany books on which can be written titles of books read, suggested and actual reading each night, and any comments that teachers and parents might wish to address to each other about children's progress. Alternatively, a little booklet, covering a longer period, might be preferred. Cards or booklets can be scanned for signs of problems requiring action and can be kept as a record.

What Response to Expect from Parents and Children

Schools should be prepared for a high level of response. One of the most consistent findings to emerge from research into this form of involvement is that virtually all parents will participate, and their participation can be maintained over a long period of time. In the Haringey Reading Project Tizard *et al.* (1982) found this level of interest and cooperation was maintained, with only two or three exceptions, by some fifty families over two years. They report that 'occasional difficulties arose as a result of housing or family problems, but again these affected only a small number of families, and in no case was contact completely lost'. In the Belfield Project parents were asked to hear their children read as often as five times a week over a three-year period. Hannon *et al.* (1985) found that the average for over seventy children who stayed three years in the school was close to four nights a week. There was some decline over the three-year period but even at the end the average was about three nights per week. Although there were no cases of parents declining altogether to participate there were a few whose participation was at a much lower rate than the average — something that was usually understandable in terms of exceptional family difficulties (Weinberger *et al.*, 1986). In a smaller scale project reported by Ashton *et al.* (1986) a level of participation just as high as in the Belfield Project was found.

Some parents can be expected to be doubtful about participating at first. A study of parents' experience of the Belfield Project found some whose very positive views about involvement had developed from an initial uncertainty or even hostility (Hannon, 1986). One said,

I think it's great, me. At first I was more surprised than anything. I'd never heard of that sort of thing before.

Another recalled,

At first I said, 'I don't get paid for teaching you', but now it's automatic.

The same study showed that the overwhelming majority of parents welcomed the opportunity for involvement provided by the project. We shall be considering the implications of this kind of evidence in Chapter 10. For the present it is only necessary to note that if a school invites parents to participate in a reading at home project it can reasonably expect a very favourable response from them. This can of course be very rewarding for the teachers concerned.

How do children respond? In view of what is known about the parents' response it can be inferred that the children like it too. It is hard to imagine how parents could maintain their involvement month after month if the children were unwilling. The children's enthusiasm rewards the adults and maintains their participation. One of the teachers in the Belfield Project described the children's response in this way (Hannon, 1986):

> At first it's very exciting for them. I think it was very important that they'd read to their parents.

The initial very high level of excitement may not last forever but it is quite reasonable for schools to count on a positive response from children that will last some time.

Anticipating and Overcoming Difficulties

As in any other aspect of school practice it pays to foresee problems. To begin with, there are what might be termed 'problems of success'. Suppose that a reading at home scheme really takes off. One immediate consequence is that children spend more time reading and will read more books. There is likely to be more wear and tear on the books (although fears of wanton damage and lost books are not usually borne out in practice). There can be difficulties if school book stocks are inadequate. Therefore it is prudent to review school and class libraries in advance and if necessary explore ways in which they can be improved. The quantity of books available for use is an important consideration but so also is their quality for that is something that will now be judged in practice, not just by one or two teachers, but by dozens of parents too.

Other problems of success can arise if a school decides to expand a scheme from small beginnings as suggested earlier. If more teachers are to participate it cannot be taken for granted that the new ones will want to work in quite the same way, and they have a right to make their contribution to the development of a scheme. Other difficulties may gradually emerge in an expanded scheme. For example, if it continues with older children there may, depending on ability, be a need for modifications for those past the reading aloud stage or others making slower progress whose interest is flagging. Record keeping procedures appropriate for a small scheme may become unmanageable with larger numbers and may need to be revised.

Sometimes difficulties arise because parents' understanding of a reading at home scheme diverges from that of teachers. For example, a scheme introduced at the beginning of the school year may go so well that at the end of term teachers decide to send books home for the school holidays too. This could come as a surprise to some parents who may prefer holidays to be a complete break from school, especially if they go away. (Some parents have similar reservations about children reading at home on fine summer evenings.) Such points can be anticipated and ways can be found of avoiding unnecessary

Table 5.2: *Implementation checklist for a reading at home scheme*

- Be aware of the strengths and limitations of initiator's role (class teacher, headteacher, outsider).
- Identify appropriate age range in the school or class.
- Choose between selective or a comprehensive strategy.
- Adopt step-by-step approach. Begin on small scale, if necessary with an arbitrarily selected group of children.
- Decide how often parents are to hear the children read. Which books are to be taken home?
- Plan how the scheme is to be presented to parents. What advice are they to be given?
- Explain the purpose and practical details of the scheme to the children.
- Devise appropriate record keeping procedures.
- Be prepared for a high level of response. If it does not materialize, don't blame the parents — instead review approach.
- Anticipate difficulties and ways of overcoming them, paying particular attention to home–school communication, impact on classroom practice, and 'problems of success'.

---

irritations by clarifying in advance, in consultation with parents, how a scheme is to operate.

Whatever the scale of a scheme, there is an impact on classroom practice that may or may not be problematic, depending upon how different class teachers look at it. A key issue is likely to be that of hearing children read in class. Some teachers accord this more importance and do it more often than others but in a situation where parents are regularly hearing children read at home some rethinking may be called for. Two responses are possible. Teachers could take the view that if parents are hearing reading there is less need for teachers to do so in class, but in practice this idea tends to make teachers rather uneasy. The difficulty is probably that teachers feel obliged to monitor children's home reading as closely as possible and to match parents' efforts. The alternative response is to hear children read in class as often as parents hear them read at home. This allows teachers opportunities for monitoring, speedier responses to parents, and up-to-date record keeping but it takes up a significant amount of time in the daily classroom routine. Some teachers may find it too time-consuming in relation to their other priorities although others, particularly teachers of younger children, may find that it fits into their practice. Different teachers will strike a balance between these factors in different ways. Anticipating this problem means recognizing that there is no single solution that suits everyone. If, in the light of experience, one approach appears unsatisfactory there are usually alternatives that can be explored.

Another aspect of teachers' practice that is likely to be changed through a reading at home scheme is the way they relate to parents. Some possible difficulties are worth noting here. An obvious one is that parents may be keener to talk about their children's reading. Some teachers might find this a little threatening, especially if parents raise some basic questions, for example about the value of having or not having structured reading scheme books, but other teachers will welcome the opportunity for an exchange of views about topics of more lasting importance than dinner money or the weather. A more serious difficulty can arise with those parents who do not participate in a scheme or whose participation is counter-productive. It must be repeated, and emphasized, that there should be very few children with such parents but even one in a class may pose a difficulty. If it is clearly undesirable for a child to take books to read at home it is often possible for some alternative in-school arrangements to be devised, for example involving a headteacher or another member of staff who might be prepared to hear the child read some time during the school day.

It is sometimes thought that parents' illiteracy might rule out this form of involvement. Illiteracy can be because English is a second language but in practice this is less of a difficulty than might be imagined. The general level of adult illiteracy in English may be quite high in some areas but even then the chances of a child having *both* parents (and *all* other members of a household) completely illiterate are low. Even then it may be beneficial for such a child to read aloud if there is someone to provide encouragement and to listen to the sense of what is said without necessarily being able to check its accuracy. A child able to read in a non-literate family could, conceivably, receive more encouragement than a child in a family where literacy is taken for granted. Many of the practical points discussed in this chapter can be summarized in the form of the checklist in Table 5.2 for those wishing to implement a reading at home scheme.

Chapter 6

A Closer Look at Hearing Reading

So far we have not delved very deeply into the nature of hearing children read apart from noting that it does require an active contribution from the teacher or parent. However, there are issues here that need to be examined more closely. If there has to be some activity on the part of the hearer, what kind of activity is most appropriate? What, in practice, are teachers' and parents' strategies in hearing children read? Are they the most appropriate ones?

Some Views about Hearing Reading

Let us begin by considering views about the purpose and practice of hearing children read. It is generally held by teachers that hearing children read is important and research clearly shows that they are prepared to make time for it in class. A national survey of over 900 primary schools, carried out for the Bullock Report, found that over half the teachers of 6-year-olds heard all the children in their class read at least three or four times a week (DES, 1975). The great majority of 'average readers' at that age (85 per cent) were said to be heard that often; almost one third were said to be heard daily. The practice was far less common for older children, except in the case of the 'poorest readers'. Other surveys of infant teachers confirm that, for young children, being heard to read in class is a significant part of being taught to read (Bassey, 1978; Gray, 1979).

Why do teachers give it this importance? In her valuable monograph, *Listening to Children Reading*, Helen Arnold (1982) suggested that one powerful reason is the widespread use of reading schemes. These require teachers to check how well children are reading particular books so that they can control, or at least monitor, their progression through the various stages of the scheme. Allied to this could be certain beliefs, which may be widely held, about the nature of reading development — that it is skill in decoding individual words and that it improves with frequent practice. Arnold also suggests that for those teachers who incline towards a child-centred educational philosophy hearing children read in class does provide the opportunity to give some time to individual children.

The Bullock Report suggested that in the early stages of reading the teacher should be 'listening to every child read several times a week' (DES, 1975). Arnold points out that this firm recommendation was something of a departure from earlier official advice about the teaching of reading in Ministry of Education publications and the Plowden Report (CACE, 1967) in which, instead, one finds more emphasis on the value of alternative techniques including silent reading. One reason for this may be that, by the time of the Bullock Report, there was an increasing concern with *diagnosis* in the teaching of reading and it is clear that oral reading can provide information to the teacher about the nature of children's reading difficulties as well as about whether they can read something. The report argued that hearing children read 'should be an essential part of the diagnostic process'. However, from a practical point of view, its discussion of diagnostic methods and their implications for action by class teachers was rather limited. This is something that has been explored in more detail, and more helpfully, by Arnold who distinguished three possible purposes in hearing children read.

> Oral reading may be used to *diagnose* how the child is progressing, to afford an opportunity for *instruction*, and what is often neglected today, to train the ability to read aloud for *communicative* purposes. (Arnold, 1982, p.36)

Diagnosis of progress through hearing reading usually means noting and analysing the mistakes children make. This can be done formally by means of a test such as the Neale Analysis of Reading Ability in which children's errors in reading particular passages are categorized into six types — mispronunciations, substitutions, refusals, omissions, reversals and repetitions. It can also be done informally, and all manner of errors can be noted. Arnold discusses such techniques but advocates the more sophisticated approach of *miscue analysis*. This was originated in the 1960s by Kenneth Goodman who argued that children's errors could reveal psychological processes involved in reading, and to emphasize that errors were not random but indicative of underlying strategies he referred to them as 'miscues' (Goodman, 1969). Arnold offers a simplified form of miscue analysis that can be carried out under classroom conditions by teachers. Children are tape recorded reading to the teacher from any passage of 150–300 words difficult enough to tax but not frustrate the child. Afterwards (presumably not in class time) the teacher examines the recording to note and code the occurrence of eight kinds of miscues — non-responses (refusals), omissions, insertions; repetitions, reversals (of words), hesitations, self-corrections and substitutions. The last of these, substitutions, are considered to be particularly revealing and are examined further to see whether they have graphophonic, syntactic or semantic similarities to the original. Arnold suggests that miscues can be positive or negative, broadly according to whether or not they indicate the child is attempting to read for meaning. Therefore one aim of the miscue analysis is to establish the overall balance between the 'positive' and 'negative'.

For diagnosis to be useful it ought to have some implications for action. Arnold suggests that from miscue analysis the teacher can identify which strategies a child needs to develop in order to make progress. A poor reader, with many 'negative' miscues, might need to be encouraged to use meaning to overcome difficulties, for example through detailed discussion of the text with the teacher. However, good readers should also be encouraged to use meaning so that, in practice, the application of miscue analysis may not make a huge difference to how different children are taught. Another implication is that parents could be encouraged to help children read for meaning without necessarily having to make detailed use of miscue analysis. There may of course be other reasons why teachers should employ it, an important one being that it may sensitize them to ways in which children learn and therefore how they may be helped.

This takes us to the second possible purpose in hearing children read — instruction. Those teachers who hear children read frequently probably do it for instructional reasons but Arnold questions the value of trying to hear children read as often as possible if this means trying to get through a class of thirty in a day, with children averaging no more than two or three minutes' individual attention. She advocates longer, necessarily less frequent, 'reading interviews' in which several activities, including reading aloud and discussion, can be shared between the teacher and an individual child.

In the third purpose that she identifies, Arnold reminds us that reading aloud can be used to develop communicative skills ('to make a clear, if not necessarily dramatic, rendering of a text for listeners'). It is worth disentangling this from other purposes that teachers have for hearing children since it is one that does not always require their attention. Arnold shows how it can form part of various group activities that children can carry out on their own, possibly freeing the teacher for individual work.

Given all these possibilities it is not surprising that some teachers have views about parents hearing children read. There is a worry that untrained non-professionals may not understand how to do it properly and that they may somehow damage young children's reading development. (This view, incidentally, is not shared by Arnold who suggests that one way to reduce the amount of hearing of reading in school is for parents to hear their children at home as in the Belfield Project.) Although hearing children read is probably the most obvious form of parental involvement in the teaching of reading there is a feeling that it is an activity requiring special skill and experience including, for example, knowledge of diagnostic techniques such as miscue analysis. Teachers may not actually want to prevent parents hearing their children read at home but they may shrink from encouraging it by sending school reading books home. One survey, referred to in Chapter 2, found that some teachers and headteachers in infant and first schools were clearly in favour of parental involvement — providing it stopped short of parents hearing their children read school reading books at home (Hannon and Cuckle, 1984). Many of the professionals had considerable doubts about parents' competence. Children might end up reading 'parrot fashion', it was claimed, or they might simply memorize books; parents might put too much pressure on children; confusion might be caused by different teaching methods; anyway, parents should let schools get on with the job of teaching. These views reflect an orthodoxy reflected in the Bullock Report's references to children receiving 'misguided teaching from over-anxious parents' and to parents 'whose efforts have been unsuccessful, or positively harmful'. Such views are not based on any firm evidence about how parents actually hear reading but only on supposition. Is there any research to which we can turn to see what happens in practice when parents hear their children read?

Research into How Adults Hear Children Read

There has been very little research into how parents do actually hear children read and how it differs, if at all, from teachers' methods. What there has been in this area has concentrated on how teachers perform in this role.

Some researchers have carried out controlled experiments to investigate whether certain strategies in hearing children read are more effective than others. In this way McNaughton and Glynn (1981) in New Zealand found that delayed, rather than immediate, attention to reading errors improves children's reading accuracy and their ability to correct errors themselves, while a study of remedial readers in the United States by Rose *et al.* (1982), has suggested that a word-supply strategy may be superior to a phonic-analysis strategy. Researchers who have studied how teachers hear children read under normal conditions have also tended to focus on certain strategies such as positive and negative feedback, or the interrupting of readers (Allington, 1980).

Several studies have been inspired by the ideas of miscue analysis and have therefore concentrated on how teachers respond to children's miscues. Spiegel and Rogers (1980) found that in a sample of Grade 2 US teachers the most common strategies in response to miscues were telling the child the correct word or assisting the child's visual perception in some way. Other strategies such as phonic analysis or reference to meaning were far less common.

There has been a series of studies by James Hoffman and his colleagues in Houston, Texas. Hoffman and Kugle (1982), using parts of an observational scheme described by Hoffman and Baker (1981), investigated how three particular teacher responses to miscues (giving no feedback, pausing, giving contextual cues) were related to teachers' beliefs about the teaching of reading and to accounts they provided of why they responded as they did. Hoffman *et al.* (1984) investigated how teacher responses were related to different kinds of miscues, children's reading attainment, and changes in attainment over a period of time.

One of the problems with research in the tradition of miscue analysis is that it naturally concentrates on how teachers respond to errors children make in reading and it tends to overlook other strategies in hearing reading which may be used whether or not errors occur. Mitchell (1980), in a detailed study that compared three teachers trained in miscue analysis with three trained in an alternative method, did consider some other strategies recommended by the alternative method and found differences between the teachers that reflected their training and theoretical frameworks. Nevertheless in this research, as in all the other studies cited so far, there is an a priori decision on theoretical grounds about what kind of hearing strategies are to be observed and then observations are carried out to determine whether, and how often, teachers use them. If we are interested in the full range of moves that parents and teachers might make, a better approach for our purposes might be to observe (and record) what happens when someone hears a child read so as to provide a general description of the activity. Such an approach cannot be entirely free of theoretical presuppositions of course but, in so far as it seeks to provide a full description of what is happening, it differs from research seeking a description within a predetermined framewrok.

An interesting attempt on these lines was made in a British study by John Gulliver (1979) who studied tape recordings and transcriptions of six teachers hearing a total of forty-one children. He used the term 'move', derived from discourse analysis, and reported finding fifty-three distinguishable moves used by teachers that he put into ten main groups according to what he thought their function might be. However, Gulliver did not provide any data on how often these different kinds of moves were used in teachers' strategies and it is difficult to judge to what extent the groups may have been derived from his expectations of the nature of teachers' strategies rather than from the observations he carried out.

Robin Campbell (1981) carried out another study in England that also used the notion of 'move' but the eight categories of teacher moves that emerged from his study of six teachers (hearing 156 children) differed significantly from those found by Gulliver. In order of observed frequency Campbell's categories were asides, feedback, directions, word recognition, comprehension, phonic analysis, providing words, and welfare. Some of these (asides, directions, welfare) do not seem to have been noted by Gulliver while others (feedback, providing words, and possibly word recognition) would probably fall into one undifferentiated category Gulliver (dismissively) termed 'conditioning'. On the other hand, some of the meaning-related moves identified by Gulliver were either ignored in Campbell's scheme or were undifferentiated within the 'comprehension' category. Nevertheless, despite these difficulties these two research studies provide a starting point.

Little comparable research has been attempted into how parents hear their children read. Stevie Hoffman (1982) has reported US research that suggested that in helping their children to read at home some parents may emphasize 'sounding out' words, and may correct children's miscues more often than is necessary and without allowing time for self-correction. Unfortunately there was no investigation of how the parents' strategies compared to those of the children's teachers. Kemp (1992) has reported on ways in which parents assisted children's oral reading but the children had reading difficulties and, again, the parents' strategies do not seem to have been compared to those of regular teachers. However, studies of the role of parents, whether working-class or middle-class, in the development of language and thinking in young children, give grounds for expecting that parents' teaching strategies in the home could compare favourably with what teachers can provide in school (Tizard and Hughes, 1984; Wells, 1985). A small scale study carried out at Sheffield by Alan Colcombe (1984) found considerable similarities in how parents and teachers heard children read. There were some indications that teachers praised more (possibly rather liberally), that children may have taken more risks with parents in attempting difficult words, and that teachers were more active in promoting comprehension. However, with just six parents and two teachers in this study, the findings can only be considered suggestive.

A Study of Parents' and Teachers' Strategies in Hearing Reading

A research study carried out at Sheffield University by Angela Jackson, Jo Weinberger and myself investigated the strategies of a larger number of parents, using a descriptive system developed for the purpose, in order to provide some hard information in an area where myths abound (Hannon *et al.*, 1986a). The parents in the study were participants in the Belfield Reading Project which tried to increase parental involvement in the teaching of reading by sending school reading books home and encouraging parents to hear their children read at home. They were given no special training but there was support and encouragement (through meetings in school, some home visiting, home–school communication by reading cards, and a general advice sheet covering the points listed in Table 5.1). There were over fifty children, taught by four class teachers, in the 5 to 7 age range in the study, from a mainly white, disadvantaged working-class population.

To find out what was happening in the reading sessions at home and in school, parents and teachers were provided with tape recorders and asked to record their children (and of course themselves) under as natural conditions as possible. Children read at home one evening, and the following day read to their teacher in class. Fortunately this procedure seemed to work quite well and some fascinating material was obtained. The study followed the approach of Gulliver and Campbell in using the concept of a 'move' to refer to the basic actions making up the hearer's activity. After reviewing tapes, and experimenting with the Gulliver and Campbell categories of moves, the Sheffield team identified the categories listed in Table 6.1. The term 'strategy' was used to refer to the pattern of moves made in hearing a child read and the idea of the research was to see whether any moves had more prominence in either the parents' or the teachers' strategies.

Table 6.1: *Moves made by parents and teachers hearing children read identified in the Sheffield study*

Moves made in response to children's miscues
    Providing negative feedback
    Insisting on accuracy
    Providing words
    Providing phrases
    Pausing
    Prompting
    Decoding — by splitting unknown word into known ones
               — by attending to initial sounds
               — by using auditory clues
               — by identifying and combining phonic elements
               — by applying phonic rules
    Encouraging use of understanding of text or context

Other moves
    Giving directions about reading
    Consolidating
    Providing positive feedback
    Praising
    Criticizing
    Establishing that child has grasped meaning
    Encouraging speculation
    Providing a reading model
    Asides

Source: Adapted from Hannon *et al.*, 1986a.

Responding to Children's Miscues

We began our examination of parents' and teachers' strategies by distinguishing moves made in response to children's miscues from those made at other points in a reading session. When children did not read accurately, it was found that there were several ways in which adults responded. These included *negative feedback* — telling the child by one means or another that a mistake has been made. For example the adult might say 'No' or some equivalent such as 'Look at it' or 'Nearly right'. Laughs and other audible responses can serve the same function. Providing negative feedback does not mean being negative towards the child; it is simply a matter of letting a reader know when inaccuracies occur. However, this is sometimes done even when the miscue is semantically acceptable. For example, a child might read 'daddy' for 'father', or 'a' for 'the' in circumstances where the substitution does not seriously affect the sense of what is being read. In such cases the adult who provides negative feedback is *insisting on accuracy* at the expense of fluency.

One of the most common responses is simply to *provide the word* (or phrase) that the child needs. On the other hand the adult might *pause* to allow a child the opportunity to work it out alone (we counted a four second wait as a pause). One can *prompt* the recall of a word, for example by saying 'You know that one' or 'You've had it before'.

Another response is to encourage the child to *decode* it by some kind of phonic analysis. Depending upon the adult's commitment to a phonics approach this would involve encouraging a child faced with an unknown word to split it up into shorter known ones (e.g. 'afternoon' into 'after' and 'noon'), to attend to the initial phoneme, to use auditory clues provided by the adult ('It sounds like . . .' or 'It rhymes with . . .'), to identify and combine phonic elements ('Split it up', 'Now put them together'), or even to apply phonic rules ('The magic "e" makes "ah" say "ay" ').

Decoding moves on the part of an adult assumes that progress can be made by tackling words singly, in isolation. In contrast, one can help the child use his or her *understanding* of the text to overcome a reading difficulty. This can be done for example by questioning the child about a relevant point, drawing attention to clues in a picture, or simply repeating nonsensical or ungrammatical miscues.

Clearly, then, there is scope for considerable variation in how adults respond to children's miscues. In our study we found that responses to miscues were a larger proportion of the parent moves (about two-thirds) than of the teacher moves (about half). In other words, parents were more likely to wait until a child was in difficulty before making a move; teachers were more likely to take initiatives at other times. However, when a careful look was taken at how they did respond to miscues, it was found that teachers' and parents' strategies were strikingly similar. For example on about 50 per cent of occasions they provided children with words or phrases. Even where there was a statistically significant difference in the use of other moves it was not particularly dramatic. So it seems that, faced with a child who hesitates or reads a word incorrectly, parents and teachers tend to respond in much the same way.

Concern for Understanding

It is widely accepted in the teaching of reading that children should be encouraged to attend to the meaning of what they read, and to use their understanding to overcome reading difficulties. Recalling teachers' worries that parents might teach children to read 'parrot fashion' or to simply memorize text, the Sheffield study looked for lack of concern for children's understanding.

Three kinds of response to miscues are relevant. Both parents and teachers made an appreciable number of moves in the category *using understanding*. It was not a very common move but there was no significant difference between teachers and parents in frequency of its use. A slightly more common response was *pause*, which shows a concern for understanding in that children are given an opportunity for self-correction or to work out words for themselves. Here again there was no difference between teachers and parents. A third category which may be relevant is *insisting on accuracy* since, arguably, this shows more concern for accuracy than for understanding. Parents did this more often. However it was still rare in comparison to moves in the other two categories so that, overall, one has to conclude that parents, in their responses to miscues, showed a concern for understanding virtually to the same extent as did teachers.

What about their moves, at other points in reading sessions, when there were no miscues? Again, we found a wide variety of moves. They include *directions* concerned with preparing for the reading session, running it, or rounding it off at the end rather than with the child's reading in itself. Some moves seem to be a matter of *consolidating* what has been learned. The child might be asked to read out selected words, phrases or passages ('See if you can remember this') or individual words might be read to the child. Providing *positive feedback* is any kind of indication, verbal ('Yes', 'That's right') or non-verbal, that the child is reading correctly. At a more general level there is *praise* or *criticism*. These moves do not provide specific feedback about accuracy of reading but communicate approval or disapproval about the child's general performance (e.g. 'Well done!' or 'You're not reading so well tonight, are you?'). There are also moves to *establish the meaning* of the text in the mind of the child, usually by questioning the child about the text or by explaining meanings. Moves to *encourage speculation* were direct invitations to the child to speculate about what might happen later in a story. Another move was to *provide a reading model* by reading a passage to the child (this could also be a response to a miscue or hesitation). Finally there were *asides* to third parties (usually other children demanding the adult's attention). Out of these, there are three kinds of move that might reflect a concern for the child's understanding.

Moves to *encourage speculation* would probably encourage children to understand what they read and moves to *establish meaning* are a very direct sign of concern for understanding. The move of *providing a reading model* could be made for a wide variety of reasons but, again, its probable effect would be to remind children that there was meaning in a text that was there to be understood. For each of these our findings were quite clear: teachers made more moves than parents.

We can summarize this aspect of parents' and teachers' strategies by saying that *both* showed a concern for understanding. For the parents, however, the concern was restricted mainly to occasions when they had to respond to a child's difficulties. Teachers, on the other hand, were more active in also trying to promote understanding at other points in a reading session.

Other Points of Comparison

There were several moves that seem to have similar importance for both groups. Giving *directions* and *providing words* were the first and second most common moves for both teachers and parents. *Positive feedback* and *negative feedback* were nearly as common and of similar importance for each. A number of less common moves also had similar importance for teachers and parents.

The Sheffield study found interesting differences too. There was an obvious discrepancy, for example, in the case of *praise* which was much more prominent in teachers' strategies. This can be seen in relation to *criticism* which was rather more prominent in the parents' strategies (although, it must be emphasized, it was still pretty rare). Many would take the view that criticism is a poor way to improve children's reading and that praise is very important in the teaching of young children but it does not necessarily follow that parents' strategies are deficient in this respect. One has to be careful here and remember the differences in the social contexts of reading at home and in school. Could it be that teachers have a less intimate relationship with children and that they may resort to praise to compensate for this, and perhaps also to keep children on task in spite of classroom interruptions? It might be artificial for parents to praise as much as teachers, and perhaps criticism from a parent is altogether less damaging than criticism from a teachers. The impression was that parents' praise when it was offered was more enthusiastic.

There were other interesting differences between children's experiences at home and in school. For example, the reading sessions at home were significantly longer — an average of about five and a half minutes at home to about three minutes in school. This points to an advantage that parents have over class teachers in hearing children read. There were also significantly more interruptions (usually from other children) in the school sessions. There was considerable variation here but the average interruption rate was about once a minute in school, against once every seven minutes at home.

Altogether, many hundreds of moves, in the various categories, were made by parents. This indicates a genuinely active involvement on their part. (They actually made more moves than teachers but this partly reflects the fact that home reading sessions were longer and, when allowance was made for this it emerged that the rate of teachers' moves per minute was significantly higher than that of parents.)

Overall Similarities in Strategies

One way in which we compared strategies overall was to take all twenty-one categories of move listed in Table 6.1 and examine how frequently parents and teachers used them in terms of their rank orders. For example, the move *providing words* was the top-ranked (i.e. the most frequent) one for both parents and teachers. The second most frequent, again for both, was *giving directions*. An infrequent move for both was *decoding by applying phonic rules* (eighteenth for teachers, nineteenth for parents). If all moves had similar prominence for teachers and parents it would suggest that they were following similar strategies. In fact there were differences — although not very great ones.

Figure 6.1 shows the rank order of the frequencies for all moves listed in Table 6.1. Moves on the diagonal of the graph have equal rank frequency for parents and teachers. *Providing words* and *giving directions*, being of first and second rank in each case, are exactly on the diagonal but it can be seen that

Figure 6.1: Relation between teachers' and parents' strategies in hearing reading in terms of their frequency of using different kinds of moves

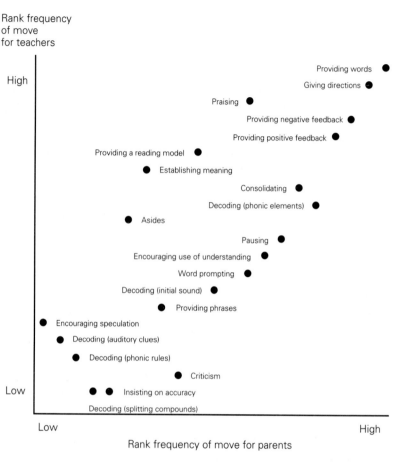

Source: Derived from Hannon *et al.,* 1986a.

many other moves were close to the diagonal (the correlation between the two rank orders, 0.78, was high). Moves that figured differently in the parents' and teachers' strategies — those lying some distance from the diagonal — have already been discussed in earlier sections of this chapter. Overall, it is reasonable to conclude that parents' strategies are very similar to those of teachers.

Implications for practice

There is obviously scope for much more research in this field involving different samples of parents and teachers and closer observation of the adult–child interaction in relation to the text. However, another study at Sheffield by French (1989) of the strategies of four more class teachers found that they were very similar to those reported by Hannon, *et al.* (1986a). The implications for practice from this study seem to be that there are no grounds for considering that parents as a group are not up to the job of hearing their children read at home. Indeed the Sheffield study suggests that parents at home have important advantages over teachers in school in terms of the greater amount of time they can spend in hearing reading, their freedom from interruptions, and their closer relationship with the children. The working-class parents in this study, despite having no training, were found to be using a wide range of moves within strategies that were similar in many respects to those of trained professionals. Therefore, in practical terms, we can probably have as much confidence in parents' abilities as in those of teachers.

However, this should not prevent us questioning parents' or teachers' strategies. Such questioning has to be rather tentative since we actually know very little about the effects of different strategies on children's long term reading development (and there are several methodological difficulties in the way of research into that issue). We have already discussed the question of whether the parents and teachers use praise as appropriately as they might. This is something that might be brought to their attention and on which they might be invited to reflect. Other questions come into view if one takes the perspective of miscue analysis. Most parents will never have heard of miscue analysis (and neither will some teachers) but, leaving aside its diagnostic possibilities, the major question it poses for hearing reading is how to encourage children to be aware of the meaning of what they read and to use their understanding to overcome difficulties. We saw that teachers were more active than parents in promoting understanding at times when children were not in difficulties. Perhaps parents could be made more aware of the relevant moves — *encouraging speculation, establishing meaning,* and *providing a reading model* — and their value might be explored in collaboration with teachers. The ways in which both parents and teachers responded to children's miscues were found to be rather similar. Their responses included meaning-related moves such as using *understanding* and simply pausing but these were far less frequent than *providing words or phrases.* We should not be too prescriptive here but perhaps both parents and teachers might reflect on the virtues of *not* immediately rushing in to help a child in difficulties. There are questions that might be asked too about the value of phonics-based decoding moves although neither teachers or parents in this study relied heavily upon them.

These questions take us to the edge of our limited knowledge about how best to help children's oral reading. Francis (1987) has pointed out how little we know. For example, we cannot be certain that the kind of help parents give children 'naturally' is the same as that resulting from a school-initiated reading project. She suggests that the latter appears 'to be very much an extension of schooling into the home' and 'it cannot be taken for granted that it will productively graft on to home-based learning' (p.224). She argues that further research, which may require some ethnography, should investigate parents' and children's intentions and understandings of the activity.

Meanwhile, in the absence of a science to provide definite rules about what is most effective, it may be advisable to treat the activity of hearing children read, like other aspects of teaching, rather as an art. Its practitioners need opportunities for intelligent reflection if they are to improve their performance. Kemp (1992) has described an Australian programme in which parents of children with reading difficulties were provided with analyses and transcripts of their reading sessions and then, through parent seminars and individual assistance, were supported in developing strategies that helped children better understand the purposes of reading. Another idea would be for adults — groups of teachers and parents — to observe each other hearing children read, using tape recordings, and then to discuss the moves they use, their likely outcomes, and alternative strategies. The descriptive system developed in the Sheffield study might provide a useful mirror, at least initially, for allowing adults to see what they are doing more clearly. Ways of describing teacher strategies and suggestions for what they should do from Arnold (1982) or Campbell (1988) might be useful too.

Just as miscue analysis can be used to improve understanding of the child's performance, so an analysis of the adult's own activity might lead to increased awareness and skill. Teacher–parent collaboration in improving strategies could be practicable, and it could be very fruitful for those concerned — provided of course that it was recognized that teachers might learn from parents, as well as parents from teachers.

Chapter 7

Other Involvement

Having looked at parental involvement in the teaching of literacy in the pre-school period and — in the teaching of reading — in the school years, in this chapter I want to discuss four other forms of involvement: 'prescriptive' approaches to hearing reading, behaviourist programmes, some in-school possibilities and 'family literacy'.

Prescriptive Approaches to Hearing Reading

The approach to parents hearing reading discussed in the last two chapters has been relatively open. That is to say, only the most general advice (e.g. on the lines given in Table 5.1) is offered to parents and it has been assumed that they will then be able to act appropriately with their children and whatever text they are reading. However, there are alternative, much more prescriptive approaches.

The most common prescriptive approach, at least in Britain, has been *paired reading*. Here the parent is shown how to read with the child, from a book chosen by the child. They begin together in a 'reading together mode', reading aloud and simultaneously. The child has to try every word. If he or she makes a mistake the parent points it out, supplies the correct word and they read it together without any further discussion. If the child wishes to read alone (the 'independent reading mode') he or she signals this (e.g. by a knock on the table) and the parent stops. The child continues in the independent mode until another mistake is made, upon which the parent points it out, allows time for self-correction and, if necessary, provides the correct word. The reading together mode is then resumed. As before, the child may revert to the independent mode. Throughout the entire procedure the parent is required to provide a stream of praise and reward, and to avoid any criticism.

The procedure was devised by Roger Morgan (Morgan, 1976) and tried out by him and Elizabeth Lyon with four families (Morgan and Lyon, 1979). It first hit the headlines when it was tried on a larger scale in the Derbyshire Paired Reading Project by Roger Bushell, Andy Miller and David Robson (1982). The Derbyshire scheme ran for eight weeks with twenty-two children. At the same time, unknown to the Derbyshire team, Alan Heath in London was carrying out an experimental study of a three-month paired reading programme for nineteen children (Heath, 1981). These studies concerned children who were considered to have reading difficulties and they measured effectiveness by using an individual oral reading test, the Neale Analysis of Reading Ability. Results suggested that a period of paired reading improved children's test scores by an amount that would normally occur over a period two or three times longer.

Paired reading differs from the simpler 'open' approaches to hearing reading in several ways. Apart from being much more prescriptive about what parents should do, it has often been directed selectively at older failing readers, it has been used for relatively short periods of time (weeks, rather than months), and it has often been evaluated by means of an individual oral reading test. The 'open' approaches have been less selective, tending to be for all younger readers in a school or class, carried on for years rather than months and evaluated by silent group reading tests.

There was continuing development of paired reading approaches during the 1980s, notably in Derbyshire (Miller *et al.*, 1986) and in Kirklees (Topping and Lindsay, 1991). Research findings from this work will be discussed in Chapter 11.

It is possible to vary details of the prescriptive approaches and to combine them in various ways. Most of the variations have been intended to help older, failing readers. They have not been taken up as widely as paired reading but they are worth mentioning because they represent distinctive alternatives, at least in theoretical terms, and in the long run one or more may become more significant.

'Pause, prompt and praise' is a method devised and first tried in New Zealand, in the Mangere Home and School Project, by Stuart McNaughton, Ted Glynn and Viviane Robinson (1981). It focuses on three aspects of what parents can do in hearing children read. When there is an error in reading, parents (and other tutors) often try to help children immediately rather than giving time to read a word or self-correct. Therefore, in this procedure, parents are asked to pause for five seconds before doing anything. After a *pause*, if the child still needs help, parents are encouraged to *prompt* a correct response in one of three ways. If the mistake does not make sense they should prompt with cues about the meaning of the story. If the mistake does make sense they should prompt with cues about the way the word looks. If the child says nothing they should ask the child to read on to the end of the sentence or read from the beginning again. If, after two prompts, the child still does not read correctly parents should simply give the word. At all stages in the procedure *praise* should be given — for reading a sentence correctly, for self-correction, or for responding correctly to a prompt. In the Mangere Project parents of eight children, aged 8 to 11, all with reading difficulties, were carefully trained to use the pause, prompt and praise procedure at home for over two months. The children's reading attainment, as indicated by the difficulty level and number of books read, improved markedly in comparison to their progress before the intervention. There were also improvements in scores on the Neale Analysis of Reading Ability test. Since the Mangere Project, the procedure has been used in other studies in New Zealand (Glynn and McNaughton, 1985).

'Shared reading' is a term used by special needs teachers and educational psychologists in Cleveland to describe a variation of paired reading in which there is only the simultaneous mode of parent and child reading together and in which parents ignore (rather than point out) any errors made by the child (Greening and Spencely, 1987). Obviously this is simpler to introduce to parents and can be used with children in all (including the very early) stages of learning to read. Although there are theoretical arguments for preferring 'shared reading' to 'paired reading' (less attention to errors, more emphasis on meaning), and it appears to have a similar effect on test scores, it has not become as well known or as widely taken up.

Other variations of paired reading have made the procedure more complex. In the Kings Heath Project in Birmingham educational psychologists used a three-stage procedure in which the simultaneous mode of paired reading was preceded by the parent reading the same text to the child, and followed by the child reading it alone, with the parent correcting errors and giving praise (Bryans *et al.*, 1985). A South Wales project tried a similar procedure except that there was a preliminary stage in which parents were asked to discuss the text and the simultaneous reading was repeated a second time with the parent allowing the child to read easier words or phrases unaided (Young and Tyre, 1983). Both procedures require repeated rereading of small sections of text and careful training of parents. There is little sign of them being taken up outside the original projects but they are an indication of how prescriptive approaches have spread and have been tried with children having considerable reading difficulties. The question of what advantage, if any, prescriptive approaches have over more open ones will be discussed in Chapter 11.

Behaviourist Approaches

The view of literacy and of literacy learning that I have taken so far in this book has emphasized the importance of meaning, and of parents helping children become literate by drawing them into meaningful literacy activities. Yet there is another view, particularly in relation to reading, that focuses on the learning of specific skills, taught (often in isolation) through structured programmes. I consider this view behaviourist in so far as it focuses on observable behaviours to the neglect of understanding and meaning which, because they are unobservable, do not figure in the vocabulary of behaviourism. Some might argue that 'pause, prompt and praise' or even 'paired reading' are behaviourist in emphasizing reinforcement through praise but there is nothing exclusively behaviourist about recognizing the importance of praise, and both of those approaches do recognize the child's efforts to construct meaning out of text. Behaviourism, on the other hand, reduces the reading process to associative learning. Procedures are far removed from any variant of hearing children read and the text used is often not even a book.

In some countries there has been a strong tradition of behaviourist approaches to teaching reading and parental involvement has meant, for example, having parents help children learn to recognize words. Sometimes the parents also administer reinforcement in the form of home rewards, privileges, or 'tokens' (e.g. Ryback and Staats, 1970; other studies in Topping and Wolfendale, 1985) but in some cases they have simply implemented learning programmes (e.g. Vinograd-Bausell and Bausell, 1987). In the UK, the PAIRS (Parent-Assisted Instruction in Reading and Spelling) project in Walsall, beginning in 1979, used the 'precision teaching' procedure. This required parents to teach children to 'read' letter sounds and words of increasing phonic complexity in programmes individually prepared by educational psychologists. At the end of each (daily) learning session parents gave children a short test (or 'probe') on what they had learned and their results were entered on a chart that could show progress over time (White *et al.*, 1984). Initially, children in the project had been referred to the schools' psychological service but later some schools in Walsall themselves involved small groups of parents in a similar way. A ten-week 'direct instruction' programme, based on the approach of Englemann *et al.* (1983), was tried by Leach and Siddall (1990) who reported significant gains for young middle-ability children.

Evaluation findings indicate that behaviourist parental involvement approaches are effective in training children to reach behavioural objectives specified in programmes. In the Leach and Siddall study there were also gains on the Neale reading test. What is less clear is whether children are helped in the long term to see the use of literacy as meaningful or enjoyable. The deep structure of this form of parental involvement is worrying too. What does it tell parents and children about literacy? There is a danger of reducing reading, for example, to learning to recognize words in lists issued from school. What do parents get from their role in behaviourist approaches? Does it empower them? Some may well learn that they have more power to teach their children than they had realized (certainly valuable in the case of children with special needs) but, more broadly, the parent is put in the role of implementing someone else's programme. Disturbingly, some the literature refers to parents as behavioural 'technicians'.

In-school Involvement

The development of involvement in the teaching of reading in Britain in the 1980s consisted in two significant shifts — from school-focused to home-focused involvement, and from indirect to direct involvement. The two went together because once parents' role at home was acknowledged its direct nature became very obvious. But is there scope for more direct involvement in school too? Leaving aside the possibility of parents serving as volunteers or classroom aides (i.e. working with children other than their own), two developments are worth mentioning: reading workshops and family reading groups.

In a reading workshop parents come into school for a regular session in which a group of them work with their own children on reading or reading-related activities with the support or guidance of teaching staff. This idea was developed in a Family Service Unit adult education project in Sheffield in 1980 and the following year was tried out fully in a one-year project at a Sheffield first school (Weinberger, 1983). This, the Fox Hill Reading Workshop, has been the best documented example of this form of involvement, and perhaps the most influential, but many other schools have worked on similar lines. Workshops include the kind of activities that many teachers might provide in class on a smaller scale without parent involvement: early reading activities, sharing books, drawing and writing, games to develop language skills, sentence building, reading-strategies, or phonic skills. In the Cambridge Parents as Tutors programme, parents spend half a session on their own, considering issues and methods in literacy teaching, and the rest of the time working with their children (Pearce, 1992).

In family reading groups parents and children come into school to read together and to share their reading experiences (Obrist, 1978). Sharing may take the form of reading to the group, reviewing particular books, discussing them, or choosing new ones from a library. The aim is to increase families' appreciation of books and enjoyment of reading which will have some effect on children's reading development. From slow beginnings outside the school system (particularly in libraries), the idea appears to be spreading in schools. Beverton *et al.* (1993) have described some possible models and indicated likely benefits for children, parents and professionals of being involved in discussing books they have read and hearing other readers' views of them. In the US, a more structured workshop approach in schools has been developed by Ruth Handel in the 'Partnership for Family Reading' programme in which parents recount reading experiences, books are presented by the workshop leader, reading strategies are demonstrated and practised, books are discussed, and parents prepare to use them at home with their children (Handel, 1992).

Family Literacy

Implicit in everything that has been said so far about children's literacy in the home and the role of parents is the *family* — the social group in which the parents' and the children's literacies meet, within which they use literacy, develop their literacy, and interact in literacy activities. Rather than treat children's literacy separate from that of parents and other members of the family, it may be more fruitful to think about the family's literacy as a whole.

The literacy that parents bring to the family will reflect their own upbringing, their personal interests and inclinations, and — crucially — how they use written language with other people outside the family in the community and workplace. The children's literacy will reflect their experiences inside and outside the family. The parents will obviously influence their children's literacy development but, because children have independent experiences (e.g. at school, in the neighbourhood, watching TV), it is also possible for their literacy to affect their parents. Family members may include either or both parents, other adults and siblings, all of whom bring their literacy practices and interact with one another in the one setting. These factors determine to what extent, and in what ways, families value literacy and how they help children to become users of written language. The family's literacy values and practices will shape the course of the child's literacy development in terms of the opportunities, recognition, interaction and models available to them. The whole is complex and would probably repay analysis as a *system* (Stafford and Bayer, 1993). Meanwhile various research studies have revealed the interplay of family literacy process in families from different social classes (e.g. Taylor, 1983; Heath, 1983: Taylor and Dorsey-Gaines, 1988) and other studies reviewed in Chapters 1 and 3 have shown the outcomes in terms of the link between children's school reading attainment and social class.

From this perspective it is clear that all attempts to involve parents in the teaching of literacy are also, to varying extents, attempts to change family literacy. Whatever the school seeks to do will be shaped, and perhaps limited, by the system of family literacy. Therefore it is the family that is the focus of intervention rather than the child, the parent or even the parent–child dyad. Where involvement depends upon parents being willing and able to change their literacy too, it obviously raises some fundamental moral and political questions about the aims of schools, methods of involvement, and what justification there may be for changing parents' literacy as well as that of children.

One way in which parental involvement programmes have had to recognize family literacy issues is in relation to parents with literacy difficulties. Some critics have used the possibility of parental illiteracy as an argument against involvement but early initiatives found, not only that such parents could help their children, but also that in some cases the parents' own literacy improved as a result of involvement (Raim, 1980; Jackson and Hannon, 1981).

In the past decade the term 'family literacy' has been used, particularly in the US, to refer not to a system that might be the focus of analysis or intervention, but to certain kinds of intervention programmes — those that aim to improve parents' literacy at the same time as improving children's literacy (either indirectly, via parents, or directly). Thus family literacy programmes have an adult basic education component combined with support for parents to interact differently with their children (in literacy and/or more generally) and perhaps also direct literacy education for the children.

McIvor (1990) has described several model family literacy programmes across the United States. Nickse (1990) has provided an overview of the research and policy background from which family literacy has emerged and the range of initiatives attempted. She offers a four-fold classification of programmes according to whether they target the adult directly and the child indirectly, vice versa, both directly, or both indirectly.

An example of a direct-adult/indirect-child programme would be the 'Parents as Readers' programme in New York (Handel and Goldsmith, 1988; Goldsmith and Handel, 1990). Adult literacy students who are parents attend workshops in which they are introduced to a range of children's books and how to use them with their children. At each workshop, one book, representative of a particular genre, is discussed and ways of reading it with children are demonstrated and then practised by the parents. Adult themes in the book are identified and some adult texts, similar to the children's books in genre, content and required reading strategy are also discussed. At home, parents try out the books and reading strategies with their children and share their experiences at the next workshop. This programme, with its concern for text and readers' responses, has a literary dimension missing in many literacy programmes (possibly because, as an adult education initiative, it started with parents and worked towards children rather than the other way around).

A very different, and extremely influential, family literacy programme has been the Kenan model (so called after the foundation which, since 1988, has supported and promoted its development from an earlier programme in Kentucky). Here parents and preschool children attend a centre several days a week. Adult basic education and parent education is provided for parents while children have good quality early childhood education (typically a High/Scope programme). Time is also set aside for parents and children to share educational experiences. The programme is intensive (e.g. three full days per week) and of long duration (e.g. a year).

Since the late 1980s, the growth of family literacy in the US, fuelled by large federal funding programmes such as 'Even Start', has been dramatic (rising to more than 1000 programmes by 1993). A National Centre for Family Literacy in Louisville, Kentucky, has taken a key role in defining and promoting a distinctive view of family literacy (with the Kenan model as the paradigm), disseminating information about practice, training staff, validating programmes, lobbying for funds and organizing national conferences attracting many hundreds of delegates. For some, these developments constitute a 'movement' (Brizius and Foster, 1993).

Family literacy has now reached Britain. In 1993 the government provided modest funds for an initiative managed by ALBSU (Adult Literacy and Basic Skills Unit) which has established five demonstration projects in different parts of the country and provided small grants for others (ALBSU, 1994). ALBSU has defined family literacy broadly as 'work with parents and children, separately and together, to improve literacy'. No single model of family literacy is being promoted at this stage but, compared with the US, British programmes are likely to be less intensive and less well-funded. It will be interesting to see what educational approaches are developed and how they balance a concern with literacy with other educational goals.

It is too early to judge the full significance of family literacy for the development of parental involvement in the teaching of literacy. It represents a considerable advance in emphasizing the intergenerational character of literacy and the power of the parent's role. It may turn out to be a more significant innovation for adult education than for early childhood education but if it attracts resources and creativity then it could provide fertile ground for developments in both sectors. However, the family literacy movement also has some worrying features.

First, it is clear that family literacy can be deeply ideological. It has emerged in the US and in Britain that right-wing governments are concerned to place responsibility for social provision, education, health and employment on the individual or the family rather than the state, and to persuade the public that this is desirable. The same governments have expressed concern about workforce illiteracy as a factor reducing industrial competitiveness. Family literacy is a neat solution to two problems — promoting families as the preferred way of meeting social needs, and at the same time promising to raise literacy levels to secure economic benefits. It both reflects and reinforces a certain ideology. The label is persuasive, for no one could possibly be against 'family' or 'literacy' singly, much less when they are joined together (it would be easier to oppose 'motherhood and apple pie'). In this context, some extravagant claims have been made:

> Family literacy can help break the intergenerational cycle of poverty and dependency. Family literacy improves the educational opportunities for children and parents by providing both learning experiences and group support. In the process, family literacy provides parents with skills that will improve their incomes. It provides disadvantaged children with educational opportunities that can enable them to lift themselves out of poverty and dependency. (Brizius and Foster, 1993, p.11)

This brings to mind Freire's comment, quoted in Chapter 1, that 'if there are not enough jobs for men able to work, teaching more men to read and write will not create them'.

A curious feature of family literacy is that when one looks closely at the content of some programmes, it is hard to find as much concern with 'literacy' or with 'family' as one might expect. For example, in the Kenan model, literacy is (quite properly) only one component of adult basic education for mothers from low-income families and literacy does not figure prominently in the children's curriculum (or in the other two key components of the model, parenting education and parent–child time together). In this programme, although not in others, 'literacy' seems to be something of a flag of convenience. Further, in so far as the programme concentrates on the mother and child rather than the father, other siblings, grandparents and so on, the term 'family' seems over-exclusive too. A better description for the Kenan model might be 'parent and child education' which is exactly what its forerunner, 'PACE', was called.

The lack of real focus on literacy goes some way to explaining what I perceive to be a theoretical vacuum in family literacy about how parents can help their children's literacy (and, at the same time, their own). In many programmes there no clear rationale for intervention or guide to what should be done (such as the ORIM framework offered in Chapter 3). Programmes such as the New York 'Parent Readers Program' (Handel and Goldsmith, 1988) or the 'Parents as Partners Reading Program' (Edwards, 1989) appear to be exceptions.

Another reason for the theoretical vacuum in family literacy may be that there has yet to be a genuine meeting of the two main traditions from which it has sprung — adult education and early childhood education. Each still concentrates on what it knows best but early childhood educators, although they have often neglected parents' learning, have generally been more concerned with *interaction* between parent and child than have adult educators. To the extent that programmes are defined and led by adult educators, rather than by a partnership between the two professional groups, the vacuum is likely to persist.

A final worry about family literacy concerns how many families it is appropriate for and how they are to be reached. The basic idea of family literacy — that teaching 'low-literacy adults' and 'at-risk children' together is better than trying to teach them separately — is intuitively very appealing. It promises 'two for the price of one'. It rests on some interlocking assumptions that turn out to be problematic when they are more closely inspected, however. It is assumes that:

1 children from families where parents have literacy difficulties are more likely than others to have such difficulties at school;
2 children who have literacy difficulties at school come from families where parents have such difficulties;
3 that by targeting families where parents have literacy difficulties we can reach children who are likely to have literacy difficulties at school;
4 that parents with literacy difficulties will be prepared to join a programme to help their children's literacy;
5 that parents with literacy difficulties are prepared to receive literacy education for themselves (as well as for their children).

Not all of these assumptions are true. To test them out we can use data from the fifth follow-up of the National Child Development Study reported by ALBSU (1993) and Bynner and Fogelman (1993). In these studies parents with literacy difficulties were those who admitted to them to interviewers; children with literacy difficulties were those whose reading test scores were in the lowest quartile.

The first assumption is true. ALBSU (1993) found, for example, that parental literacy difficulties, coupled with low family income, meant that children had a 72 per cent chance of being in the lowest reading level (compared to 25 per cent for children as a whole). However, it does not follow that the second assumption is true. In fact it is not — the vast majority of children in the lowest reading level did *not* have parents who admitted to literacy difficulties. It follows that the third assumption is false. Parental literacy difficulty cannot be used to identify all the children who are likely to have literacy difficulties in school and who would therefore benefit from early intervention — it misses too many children. (Even amongst those it does identify, it will turn out to be wrong in about 30 per cent of cases.) The fourth assumption is probably true — studies of parental involvement show that almost all parents, including those with literacy difficulties, are prepared to participate in programmes that they believe will help their children. The fifth assumption is much more questionable. Bynner and Fogelman (1993) found that 'less than one-fifth of those who reported literacy problems had attended an adult literacy class' (p.57). It may therefore be an uphill struggle to persuade parents to attend literacy education for themselves and, if that is made a condition of admission to a programme, family literacy will not reach targeted children.

The alternative to family literacy is good, literacy-oriented early childhood education (including preschool education) for broad groups of families likely to benefit. It should maximize parental involvement and provide opportunities for adults to develop their literacy too if they want to. That is a much more expensive — and therefore at the present time politically less attractive — option than family literacy which claims to achieve the same more cheaply. In the long run, family literacy divorced from early childhood education may be difficult to sustain. Meanwhile, schools have much to learn from the ideas and methods being tried with families.

Chapter 8

The Need for Evaluation and Research

The ideas and arguments put forward in this book have rested heavily on research but I believe there are deficiencies in both the quality and the quantity of studies currently available to us. The problem mainly concerns what I call *evaluation* or *evaluative research* rather than what I call *theoretical research*. Therefore in this chapter I want to offer a view about what evaluation is, what it should accomplish, and how findings from evaluation studies should be shared within the education community.

The Nature of Evaluation

Innovation in education ought to be accompanied by evaluation — without it, we are at the mercy of prejudice or educational fashion. Evaluating parental involvement in the teaching of literacy means identifying what forms of involvement, if any, are valuable so that they can be developed further and taken up more .widely. The following chapters will look at two basic approaches to evaluation in this field, what may be termed 'evaluation by tests' and 'evaluation by participants'. This will enable us to go on later to ask, 'What has been learned so far?' However, my aim here is first to set out some key ideas that should inform how we think about evaluation in general.

One quite fundamental idea is that *evaluation is to do with values* that underlie the aspirations and goals for which teachers, parents and others strive in education. Many goals are widely held in society (e.g. that children should understand what they read, that school leavers should be able to spell) but conflict arises because people attach higher values to some goals than to others (e.g. in early childhood education, relative importance of reading for meaning versus the early acquisition of phonic skills). The problematic nature of values is often glossed over in evaluation by focusing on particular outcomes such as children's 'reading ages' as indicated by some test as if that were self-evidently the most valued aspect of the innovation.

A second key idea is that *evaluation is to help us choose between options* — to involve parents or not, to involve them in this way or that — and we want to know the value of opting for one course of action rather than another. Unless there is some possibility of doing things differently there is no practical point in carrying out an evaluation. Sometimes the alternatives may be implicit but it is nearly always more helpful if an evaluation can make them explicit. One of the strengths of experimental designs is that the alternatives have to be made explicit in the form of 'control' or 'comparison' conditions. For example, the value of an at-home reading programme might be compared to doing absolutely nothing with parents or to putting equal effort into, say, an in-school reading workshop initiative. Qualitative methods are often needed to reveal the meaning of different options.

Third, *evaluation ought to concern the costs as well as the benefits* of innovation. It is foolish to deny that work with parents costs time and possibly other resources too. One form of involvement may appear more valuable than another in terms of a particular measure of children's reading progress but it may be too costly, for example, in terms of teacher time or because it has a disabling effect on parents. If the evaluation considers other options, their costs ought to be noted too. It may then turn out that an innovation saves time and resources in comparison to an alternative (e.g. providing remedial reading support). Obviously, values can apply to costs as well as benefits.

Fourth, evaluation should not be confused with research or, more accurately, *evaluative research is not the same as theoretical research.* The fact that the two enterprises often use the same designs and techniques such as interviewing, tests or ethnography can mislead us into thinking that one is much the same as the other. The agenda for theoretical research in literacy or parental involvement should be determined by the needs of theory development — the ultimate aim being to build a system of interconnected concepts and generalizations or at least to understand things better. Often this means focusing on the relation between one or two factors and, although these could be of immediate practical relevance, they need not be. In the long term, good practice does need sound theoretical underpinning but, in the short term, research to advance theory may not be all that helpful practically. Evaluative research, however, ought to be focused on the problem of choosing between given options ('Is A more valuable than B?') and, rather than isolating one or two factors, it usually has to take a holistic view of a situation. Given this distinction, one has to be wary of using theoretical studies for evaluation purposes and vice versa. It is sometimes thought that evaluative research can afford to be less rigorous and it is certainly true that compromises often have to be made (e.g. in sampling). On the other hand, it is not generally appreciated that evaluation often has to be *more* rigorous. For example, in theoretical research, one may be able to make allowances for limitations in the construction of a reading test which it would be quite disastrous to use for evaluative purposes.

Finally, *evaluation is for teachers.* It is their practice that is to be developed and, ultimately, only they can develop it. It follows that evaluation has to be intelligible and illuminating for teachers. Otherwise it might as well not be carried out at all. Whenever possible, teachers themselves should be the ones to do the evaluating. Of course they cannot possibly be formally evaluating every aspect of their practice all the time. Therefore they have to make use of studies reported by others, provided that their relevance can be judged from information provided in the reports.

Two Approaches to Evaluation

From this perspective it is not at all obvious that parental involvement in the teaching of literacy should be evaluated solely, or even principally, by children's test performance. Yet this is what has happened in Britain. Involvement made headlines in the 1980s because of claims about reading test results, and tests are what most people turn to when they think about evaluation — an obvious way, it seems, to find out 'what works'. This may be a legacy of pioneering studies in the field such as the Haringey Project and the Derbyshire Paired Reading Project. These were certainly concerned with the development of practice, but they had a theoretical orientation too, and made use of tests within a psychological research tradition. Evaluation that is focused more closely on practice and less concerned with theory development does not have to do the same.

The alternative to test-based evaluation is to give more weight to the experiences, activities and views of the main participants — parents, teachers and children. This may require direct observations, record keeping, interviewing, and careful reflection on what a programme means in operation to those most closely involved. The two main approaches — which need not exclude each other — are discussed in Chapters 9 and 10.

The Reporting of Evaluations

If what is learned in an evaluation is to be shared with teachers and others elsewhere then obviously the evaluation has to be reported in some way, and the report published. Without a report, whatever is learned from an evaluation is confined to those involved in carrying it out at a particular time and place. Unfortunately, the content of evaluation reports and the way they are published often leaves a lot to be desired. Misleading reports, and misleading accounts of reports, have for example overstated the benefits of some forms of involvement to the long term detriment of good practice.

A good report needs to make it clear why the evaluation was carried out — which questions it addressed, and which ones it did not address — so that people not directly involved can see how it might be relevant to their situation. All too often this preliminary is seen as unproblematic by evaluators who proceed to interview parents or administer tests to children without regard to the aims of the programme in question. It is also vital that the nature of the parent involvement programme is described fully enough so that teachers or others elsewhere could try the same thing themselves. The main aspects to consider here — target group, objectives, duration and method — are the ones that were discussed in some detail in Chapter 2 and listed in Table 2.1.

A test-based evaluation report should recognize problematic aspects of using tests and therefore explain why a particular test was used, how children's performance on that test might indicate reading competence, how closely it matches what they do in the programme, and, if standardized scores or 'reading ages' are used, how well the test was standardized. The kinds of test measures used (raw scores, post-test scores, or pre-test–post-test gains) should be made clear.

Some awareness of the problems of research designs should inform any evaluation report. At the very least it should be made clear which of the principal alternative designs was chosen, and why. In the case of experimental designs, control conditions need to be specified in enough detail for people elsewhere to judge whether they would have the same starting point were they to introduce a similar programme.

Although it is not reasonable to expect an evaluation to report all test data collected, there ought ideally to be enough detail for readers of a report to decide for themselves whether they would have reached the same conclusions as the evaluators. For example, if mean test scores are quoted so should the standard deviation, number of children tested, and perhaps the range of scores. If differences in mean scores or differences in percentages reaching certain test levels (say, between experimental and comparison groups) are quoted then statistical tests for checking how likely it is that such differences could have arisen by chance should be applied and details provided. In the case of qualitative evaluation one needs to know whose views are reported and under what conditions, which participants were not interviewed, and what kind of data was left 'on the cutting room floor'.

The final stage in carrying out an evaluation is *publication* of a report. This can take many forms and there can be variations in the degree to which a report is genuinely publicly available. There can be also be a relation between the form of publication and the quality of the evaluation. For example, it is not commonly appreciated outside the academic research community that reports published in research journals such as the *British Educational Research Journal* are subjected to a refereeing process. This usually means that two or more workers in the field will have checked a report's methodology, data analysis, relation to other studies and the soundness of any conclusions reached. Many papers submitted to research journals fail this process and are rejected outright or returned to authors for improvements. Refereeing does not guarantee that every study published is a good one but it does at least decrease the chances of poor ones getting through.

Some journals do not have formal refereeing procedures and publication is more likely to depend upon the editor's judgment of what will interest readers while maintaining the journal's standing. For others, particularly news-papers such as the *Times Educational Supplement*, results of an evaluation may only be published if they are newsworthy or controversial. The sound-ness of an evaluation may be a minor factor in the decision to publish and the text written by authors can sometimes be extensively revised by subeditors. Newspapers often give incomplete or distorted accounts of research findings which makes it all the more necessary that teachers have access to a proper evaluation report.

Teachers may find it difficult to have evaluations published by journals or periodicals, which can operate as a barrier to sharing ideas within the educa-tional community as well as channels for communication. In Britain, the *Class-room Action Research Network Bulletin* has been an attempt to provide an alternative forum for the exchange of ideas. Also there are some journals that make a particular effort to publish articles by teachers (e.g. *Education 3–13, Reading, Cambridge Journal of Education, Educational Action Research*).

Some form of self-publication is another solution and many schools and agencies have produced booklets, or modestly printed reports, for sale or distribution to those who are interested. These efforts are to be welcomed but they are not without problems. There is no outside check on the standard of the evaluation or the extravagance of claims for its importance (the preface to one such report announced that it would 'do for community education what *Origin of the Species* did for evolution'). Also, such reports may still not be really published in the sense of being genuinely publicly available. A test for genuine publication of a report is whether or not a copy can be obtained through a public or higher education institute library. If only a few people have access to a report others cannot use it or check for themselves what is said about it. A solution is to use the US-based information service, ERIC (Educational Resources Indexing Centre) to which authors can send reports to be made available on request. If a report is well-presented and likely to be of interest ERIC will store information about it in its series *Resources in Education* or on its computer data-base and teachers throughout the world can locate it and obtain a paper or microfiche copy directly or through libraries.

Finally, it is possible to publish a report as a book or as a substantial section of a book. This has advantages from the point of view of dissemination but it can sometimes give an unjustified authority to research. The Radical Statistics Education Group in 1982 produced a detailed critique of research design inadequacies in some influential studies of school effectiveness. They had all been published as books and the group commented as follows:

> Research published in book form tends to escape the scrutiny of pro-fessional peers in a way that research reported in academic journals does not. There is something to be said for publishing at least some of the research findings in journals before writing a book although this can lead to some frustrating delays. (Radical Statistics Education Group, 1982, p.31)

A problem with reports in the field of parental involvement in the teaching of reading has been 'hype', which the group defined as 'the promotion of a product beyond its intrinsic merits, in these cases by overselling and dropping qualifications' (p.27). Sometimes this happens because writers have sought publicity; sometimes because the press has exaggerated reports. To combat it, the group argued that researchers should ensure that the conclusions of their reports avoid hype and that they try to anticipate later debate in the media by stating clearly which recommendations are warranted by the research and which are not.

It would be easy to become cynical about the quality of educational research and the claims of evaluation reports but that would be going too far. What is needed is healthy scepticism rather than cynicism. Reports, like all other texts that seek to describe or persuade, need to be read *critically*. As the Radical Statistics Education Group pointed out, 'ultimately, the only defence against hype is a confident and critical readership' (1982, p.28). If we are to learn from evaluation it is not enough to accept at face value claims of the form 'numerous reports show . . . such and such'. One needs to know exactly what kind of involvement was evaluated, the quality of the evaluation and reporting, what checks, if any, there were on the reports, and whether they are genuinely publicly available. Not all reports are of equal value by these criteria. The quality of reports and the way in which they are published will determine whether or not evaluation shapes the future development of practice in involving parents.

Evaluation in Context

Although evaluation is indispensable in the development of good practice it needs to be kept in perspective. The effort put into evaluation should only be part of the effort put into involvement. Only in exceptional cases should all of the possible evaluation methods be fully used. In many schools, limitations of time, energy and expertise mean that evaluation can only consist of the minimum demanded by good practice. In others, where it is felt that some extra effort to evaluate is necessary, a judgment will have to be made about which of these methods are appropriate and can be afforded. We need to develop an enlarged view of how parental involvement in the teaching of literacy can be evaluated. *Test-based evaluation* is one way but it is more difficult and less helpful than is widely believed. *Evaluation by participants* provides a broader, more practical and probably more helpful way of identifying what is valuable practice. However, it is to be hoped that, whatever level of evaluation is undertaken, there will be a conscious review of *all* the possibilities available rather than an uncritical reliance on any one of them.

Also, it should be remembered that it is most unlikely that the question of whether or not to involve parents, or which form of involvement is best, will be settled by evaluation alone. Other social, political and educational forces are often more powerful. Therefore the function of evaluation in relation to parental involvement is a modest, formative one of steering it clear of pitfalls and in more rewarding directions for all concerned rather than anything more ambitious or summative. With this in mind we can turn to a more detailed consideration of test-based evaluation.

Chapter 9

Evaluation by Tests

To assess how tests can be used in evaluation — and, just as important, how they can be misused — it is necessary to clarify two problematic issues: the nature of test performance and the validity of research designs using test data.

Test Performance

In the following discussion, the focus will be on reading tests. There are many more of these than writing tests because of the prominence that reading has always had in the curriculum and in the popular view of what counts as literacy. It also reflects the narrower range of possibilities in testing writing. There are several different ways of testing reading (individual oral reading tests, word recognition tests, silent group sentence-completion tests, and so on). For writing, the possibilities are limited to dictation or writing a text for some contrived purpose. The former is hardly more than a spelling test; the latter is difficult to standardize and measure.

What do reading tests measure? What can test scores or 'reading ages' really tell us about the benefits of parental involvement? To answer these questions let us use a distinction that has been found useful in other areas of language research, between *competence* and *performance*. Reading competence can be thought of as true reading ability — the sum of everything a child can do in relation to reading. Competence is what teachers and parents value and seek to improve but of course it is not something that can be observed directly. All that can be seen is reading performance in one situation or another. We can try to use performance as an indication of competence but we can never be certain that, in any given situation, a child has the opportunity to perform to the full extent of his or her competence. The basic problem with all reading tests is that they rely on performance on one particular artificial reading task to indicate children's competence across many real-life tasks.

In other areas of child development researchers have come to accept that children's performance on artificial tasks can be a misleading indicator of their competence. For example, tasks devised by Piaget to test young children's logical competence were shown some years ago to pose hidden difficulties that lowered performance (and led to underestimates of competence) more than better-designed tasks (Bryant, 1974; Donaldson, 1978). In the area of language, the once too-widely assumed deficiency in the competence of working-class children tended to disappear as researchers studied their performance in situations where extra, artificial demands were removed (Edwards, 1976; Wells, 1978; Tizard and Hughes, 1984).

The construction of reading tests is a problematic business. The usual approach is to devise some activity or task that resembles reading activity and on which one can measure performance fairly easily. A child's score can then be related to some criterion of achievement or to norms for his or her age group.

In the early tests devised by Burt and Schonnell (see Pumfrey, 1985), children were shown a list of words of increasing difficulty and were asked to read them out. The more they read correctly, the better the test score (and the older the age of children for whom that was an average score, the higher the 'reading age'). But what is the relation between this kind of test performance and reading competence? There is obviously some relation but it may not be a very strong one. In most real-life reading we do not just read single words in isolation and we do not read them aloud. Also, there is more to reading than decoding. Reading involves getting meaning from text and it is possible to decode perfectly in the sense of producing the appropriate sounds for words without understanding anything. Therefore good performance on this reading task does not necessarily indicate a high level of competence. Likewise, poor performance may be due not to a low level of reading competence but to some other factor such as a child's speech difficulties in front of the tester or a poor match between the child's vocabulary and the words chosen to make up the test.

Instead of single words children can be given passages of text to read aloud and certain tests such as the Neale Analysis of Reading Ability (Neale, 1966) do require that kind of performance. In some ways this is an improvement, for children can use the meaning of the text to help them read it in the way that mature readers do, and the children can be questioned on their comprehension of what they have read, which tests another important aspect of reading competence. Some problems persist, however, in that a child's speech difficulties or vocabulary may still depress performance, and new problems arise from trying to make the task meaningful. A child's comprehension of any text depends, not just on their reading competence but on their prior knowledge of whatever the text is about and that, in turn, can depend on cultural background as some studies have demonstrated (Steffensen *et al.*, 1979; Reynolds *et al.*, 1982). It has been argued that the resulting distortion in tests of reading comprehension can only be reduced by measuring the extent of individuals' prior knowledge (Johnston, 1984). However, this is difficult so children's prior knowledge is, in practice, an uncontrolled variable affecting both reading comprehension and the accuracy of reading aloud. In the case of the Neale test this could be a serious problem; in one study of poor readers who had the passage read to them it was found that their reading comprehension age was still more than two years behind their chronological age (Pumfrey and Lee, 1982).

Another kind of task devised for reading tests is to read words out to the child who then has the task of identifying them amongst several others printed on the test paper, e.g. the Southgate word recognition test (Southgate, 1959). Although this certainly requires some reading competence it is just one particular aspect amongst those called for in real life. Again it deals with single words in isolation. It does not make any demands on children's speaking ability but their hearing and memory capacity could affect their performance.

There are some reading tests that are entirely silent and that require children to read sentences or passages — for example, sentence-completion tests like Young's or NFER Reading Text A in which children have to choose a word or phrase to fill a gap in a sentence (Young, 1980; NFER, 1973). These are much better because the test activity is closer to true reading. Children have to use their understanding, and that reflects the essential meaning-getting aspect of reading competence. But again, there is the problem that how well children understand the text in the test depends on factors apart from their reading ability. For example, if their cultural background differs significantly from that of the test constructor, children might understand some sentences differently or others might not make any sense at all. A study I carried out with Joe McNally demonstrated this in the case of NFER Reading Test A (Hannon and McNally, 1986). We found that even when the tester read out the incomplete sentences and the alternatives that could go into the gaps some children from working-class or ethnic minority backgrounds still gave 'incorrect' responses (although these might have been correct from their cultural perspective). Clearly, children's performance on this test was not simply a reflection of their reading competence.

A fundamental problem with reading tests can be stated thus. Those tests in which the performance requires children to use their understanding can easily amount to a test of culture. Yet those that do not require understanding can scarcely be considered tests of reading competence at all.

What does this mean for using reading tests in the evaluation of parental involvement? There must be some doubt about whether parental involvement should be expected to boost reading test performance. It might be worrying if involvement depressed performance but we should only be looking for gains where it is clear that the test performance is a valid indication of some aspect of reading competence that it is our goal to improve. Otherwise, if the value of parents' involvement is assessed solely by its power to raise scores on a certain test and no gains result, there is a risk of concluding there has been no effect when the benefits may have been in another area.

Tests can also mislead if there is too close a *match* between the test performance and the parental involvement programme. For example, if the programme means a large increase in how often children read aloud to their parents then an individual oral reading test (in which they read aloud to an

Table 9.1: Examples of tests used in the evaluation of parental involvement in the teaching of reading

NATURE OF TEST PERFORMANCE	NAME OF TEST	USED BY
Silent reading of sentences — identification of missing words or phrases. Group test.	NFER Reading Test A	Tizard *et al.* (1982); Ashton *et al.* (1986); Hannon (1987).
Silent reading of sentences — identification of missing words. Group test.	Young's Group Reading Test	Tizard *et al.* (1982); Hannon (1987).
Oral reading of passages to an adult. Answering of comprehension questions. Individual test.	Neale Analysis of Reading Ability	Bushell *et al.* (1982); Lindsay *et al.* (1985); Miller *et al.* (1986); Leach and Siddall (1990). Most paired reading studies reviewed by Topping and Lindsay (1992).
Silent reading of short texts — identification of missing words. Group test.	Hunter-Grundin Literacy Profiles	Widlake and Macleod (1984)
Oral reading of sentences to an adult. Individual test.	Holborn Reading Test	Greening and Spencely (1987)
Word recognition. Silent reading of sentences — identification of missing words. Group test.	Primary Reading Test	Ashton *et al.* (1986)
Silent reading of passages — identification of missing words, answering comprehension questions. Group test.	London Reading Test	Hewison (1988)

adult) is obviously quite likely to show an improvement. The children have, in effect, been practising the kind of performance required by the test. On the other hand a silent sentence-completion group test (in which the test performance differs in almost every respect from the child's activity with the parent) is less likely to be directly affected by children reading to parents so, if there is an effect, it is something to be taken more seriously. Table 9.1 lists some reading tests that have been used in research and evaluative studies of parent involvement. The tests require different kinds of performance, some of which match a given programme of involvement better than others.

A close match between programme and test performance is not always a weakness in evaluation design. It all depends on programme objectives. If a test is a valid indication of whether those objectives have been met then there can be no objection to it being used. 'Teaching to test' is not necessarily a bad thing. However, in practice, most tests require a narrow range of performance and it is unlikely that many parent involvement programmes would have similarly narrow objectives. The important point in judging the suitability of a test is to be aware of exactly what performance it requires and therefore which objectives it can be used to evaluate.

This assumes that some thought is actually given to the choice of a test. Unfortunately this aspect of test-based evaluation is not usually given the attention it deserves. Most users of tests are not very interested in how they are constructed, the nature of the task performance, how the test was standardized or even whether it ever has been standardized. They may even have an aversion to considering such issues. Busy teachers want something they can use straight away. Researchers too, whether they be teachers or specialist evaluators, tend to be more interested in the programme they are studying than the means used to evaluate it. Consequently the choice of test may depend on what other people in the same situation appear to have done, on a colleague's recommendation, or on what happens to be in the cupboard at the time. There is also a commercial aspect to tests that discourage users from using the most appropriate. They are difficult to view without buying; yet they are often too expensive to buy for inspection purposes. Publishers are not always helpful in pointing out the limitations of their products. The answer is to consult a guide to tests (e.g. Vincent *et al.*, 1983; Pumfrey, 1985) and allow time and money for getting the least worst one. Any test-based evaluation study should provide a justification for the test chosen.

Research Design

Obtaining a set of test scores for children in a parent involvement programme is not the end of the evaluator's problems for, even if the test is well chosen, what does one do with the test scores? They have to be compared to something or else they are meaningless. But to what? The various ways of finding comparisons have been explored within the theory of research design, or at least that part of it which relates to experimentation and quasi-experimentation.

One could compare children's test scores at the end of an involvement programme to how they did on the same, or a related, test before it began. This is sometimes referred to as a 'one-group pre-test/post-test design' (Campbell and Stanley, 1963). A moment's reflection shows its weakness for there is no way of knowing whether or not any gains in test scores would have happened anyway. If there are no gains, or if there are losses, there may be cause for concern but it is still impossible to infer anything about the positive or negative value of the programme because other factors may be at work too.

Suppose, however, that the test scores are not simple measures of performance (raw scores) but standardized in a way that shows how each child stands in relation to norms for his or her age level (e.g. centiles, standardized scores, 'reading ages', 'reading quotients'). The performance of children in the programme can now be compared to that of other children in the standardization sample in one of two ways: in terms of post-test scores (i.e. post-programme scores) or in terms of pre-test/post-test gains (the change in test scores pre-programme to post-programme).

An example of a post-test scores comparison with a standardization sample is provided by Widlake and Macleod (1984). They attempted to evaluate the impact of the Coventry Community Education Project on school 'reading standards'. From schools in the project, over 700 children in six selected schools were tested with the Reading for Meaning Scale from the Hunter-Grundin Literacy Profiles. Older children in the project scored distinctly above national norms, young children below. In effect Widlake and Macleod used the test standardization sample as a kind of control group — a group of children who had not received whatever was provided in the Community Education Project.

This design focuses attention on the way in which the test was standardized, details of which could be found in the test manual (Hunter-Grundin and Grundin, 1980). This tells us that the norms were based on test results of over 2800 children in seventy schools selected to be representative of the variation in schools in twenty-three LEAs. This procedure would be quite adequate for most purposes but, if the standardization sample is to be treated as a control group, more information is needed. When was the standardization carried out? Who selected the schools and by what criteria? What evidence is there that, in the end, it was a representative sample? This information is not provided but an interesting and valuable feature of the test manual is that it gives mean scores found for 'working-class' and 'educational priority area' schools in the standardization sample. Using these as a basis of comparison, Widlake and Macleod argued that schools in their project were doing even better. This is, however, asking much more of the standardization procedure than it was designed to bear. The test manual does not tell us how many of the seventy schools were in each category or how they were categorized as 'working-class' (rather than 'middle-class' or 'mixed'). Criteria for disadvantaged schools can vary between areas or from one time to another. Another difficulty is that the method of testing or marking in the standardization procedure may have differed from that in the evaluation study. Indeed Widlake and Macleod acknowledged that most of their testing was done by the research team (instead of teachers as in the standardization procedure) but argue that this was a deviation 'in the direction of greater rigour'. Whether or not it was more rigorous, it was a deviation, and it could either improve or depress test scores of children in the project. In summary, relying on test norms — even relatively sophisticated ones — for comparative purposes is a very uncertain way to evaluate a programme.

An alternative is to use *gains* in standardized scores. It is an improvement on the simple one-group pre-test/post-test design for, instead of looking at changes in raw scores between the start and end of a programme, one can see whether children have changed more or less than children in the standardization sample changed over the same period of time. Again, this is using the standardization sample as a kind of control group. For example, over a one-year programme, a change in mean raw scores from 17 to 24 on a given test may seem a gain but it could represent more or less than the average difference in raw scores for children one year apart in age. If the children's scores were expressed in a standardized form this could mean, for example (to use norms from an actual test) a change from 101 to 94 — clearly a drop. On the other hand an increase from 17 to 44 could (referring to the same test) mean a gain in standardized score from 101 to 109. Children normally perform better at reading tests as they get older; using standardized scores automatically tells us whether the improvement in the group's score is more or less than the norm. Or does it? Once again there is the difficulty of ensuring that the conditions of testing in the standardization procedure and in the evaluation are the same although, since the comparison is in terms of pre-test/post-test gains rather than post-test scores alone, it may be sufficient to ensure simply that there is no change in testing conditions from pre-test to post-test. A more awkward difficulty concerns the timing of testing. The programme to be evaluated might run from the beginning of one term to the end, or from the beginning of one school year to the end; that is, the period of a programme can be between various points in the cycle of the school year. It is quite likely that children's reading improves more quickly at some periods in the school year (e.g. in the first or second term) than at others, and it may even decrease during some (e.g. the summer holidays). These irregularities cannot be reflected in test norms because the standardization procedure is often carried out at one point in the year and the difference, say, between the seven years, two months level and the seven years, four months levels is not between the same children at those ages but between all of those at one age and all of those at the other at the time of testing. A further, and in practice more serious, difficulty is the age range of the test. Because children differ so widely in reading attainment it is difficult to devise reading tests that are suitable for all abilities. The danger is either that they will be too hard so that the least able cannot score at all or not hard enough so that there is a ceiling to scores for the most able, or both. This difficulty is increased if the ability range is widened by using the test at both ends of a period of time. Not all tests can span the full ability range over a period as long as a year although that may be quite a short period of time for a parent involvement programme. Obviously, if one resorts to different tests at the beginning and end of the programme the advantages of a pre-test/post-test design are lost.

There are, then, many difficulties in using standardization data for comparative purposes in test-based evaluation. The difficulties become less when the characteristics of the standardization sample and the way it is tested approximate to a control group, so let us now consider the proper use of *controls* in test-based evaluation. The ideal way of using them is in a true *experimental design*. This means having two groups of children that differ only in that one, the experimental group, receives the programme whereas the other, the control group, does not. Any differences in test performance at the end can be attributed to the programme or purely to chance (and the probability of chance variations can be estimated statistically). The basic idea is very simple and widely understood. In the right circumstances an experimental design can provide clear cut answers to the kinds of questions asked in evaluation but there are ways in which its strengths can be lost if one is not careful.

It is crucial that everything is done to reduce the likelihood of differences between the experimental and control groups except in the 'treatment' they receive during the period of evaluation. The ideal procedure is to have a sample of children or parents and allocate them to the experimental or control groups *strictly at random* (e.g. by picking names out of a hat, using random number tables or by a computer programme). This cannot entirely eliminate differences between groups but it does mean that any such differences are due to chance and their extent can therefore be estimated statistically. Evaluators are often tempted to 'improve' on this procedure, for example, by creating a control group of children matched to children in the experimental group on certain characteristics. Despite its attractiveness this procedure is inferior to random allocation (although it might be better than having no controls at all). Matching has two weaknesses. First, one can never be certain that the characteristics chosen for the matching are the crucial ones in relation to the programme or the test performance. Second, because there is an element of judgment in deciding on each match, there is the possibility of introducing some systematic bias — possibly unconscious — that will produce non-random differences between the two groups which will affect test performance. If random allocation is possible then it is usually not worth losing its statistical benefits by introducing matching.

Random allocation can be difficult in practice. It might mean, for example, picking out certain children in a class and working with their parents while their classmates are not included in the programme. It is usual to treat all children in a class in much the same way so special treatment for some children may not be acceptable to the class teacher; it may cause comment and it may in itself have effects — either positive or negative — on those included or those excluded. Another difficulty is that, if one believes the programme is likely to be beneficial for the children concerned then allocating some children to the control group seems like denying them a benefit. This difficulty arises, of course, with any potentially beneficial innovation in education unless it is introduced universally from the start — it is simply more obvious in an experimental design. Neither difficulty should be assumed to be insuperable. Their seriousness needs to be carefully assessed in the context of the particular programme to be evaluated. One strategy that can meet both difficulties if the programme is not too long is to provide it for the control group after the experimental group has completed it. The evaluation can cease when the experimental programme ends or it can sometimes be usefully extended to monitor the control group's experience of the programme too.

Very few evaluations of parental involvement in the teaching of literacy have used true experimental designs. Often the 'control groups' have not been created by random allocation but are parallel or earlier classes, or cohorts, of children in a school or children at a different school. We shall refer to these as 'comparison groups' rather than control groups. Following Campbell and Stanley (1963) these designs are termed *quasi-experimental.* Their weakness is that there are more differences between the experimental and comparison groups than the fact that one receives the programme and the other does not. For example, children may have been allocated to one class or another, not at random, but to satisfy the needs of school organization. If school staff attempt to produce equivalent classes from the class teacher's point of view they may consciously or unconsciously use criteria that produce different groups from the evaluator's viewpoint. The fact that different classes have different class teachers is itself a factor of obvious importance — one teacher may be more effective than another in teaching reading or working with parents or both. If the comparison group is an earlier class, to be used as a 'baseline' against which the programme class performance is to be compared, then there is a danger that other things in the school, apart from the introduction of the programme, may have changed since the baseline performance was measured. The problem common to all quasi-experimental designs is that there are un-controlled, often unknown, variables which may distort the effects of parent involvement.

This does not mean that quasi-experimental designs are useless. The important point is to be aware of their limitations and to take these into account in interpreting and generalizing from results. Also, it is sometimes possible to compensate for weaknesses in a design. For example, if there are doubts about whether the experimental and comparison groups are similar in reading achievement at the start of a programme then a pre-test could be given to both groups and, if no significant difference is found, the level of doubt may be reduced (a check that is not strictly necessary in a true experimental de-sign). If there are doubts about whether a programme's results are due to teacher efforts it may be possible to replicate the evaluation with experimental and comparison teachers exchanging roles. It may be possible to allocate classes at random to experimental or comparison conditions although for this to 'control out' teacher efforts there has to be a large enough number of classes to reap the statistical benefits. If there is a baseline–programme design then doubts about the effects of factors that vary over time may be reduced by having baseline and comparison groups extending over several years or hav-ing a baseline–programme–baseline sequence.

One problematic issue that affects both experimental and quasi-experimental designs is the nature of the non-programme conditions for the control or comparison groups. What is the alternative to which involvement is to be compared? It is not sufficient simply to say that control/comparison children have nothing at all. Children in the experimental group are not only having parental involvement but may be receiving extra attention or resources. They have the novelty and excitement of something special which in itself, quite apart from its specific nature, may have an effect. This is sometimes referred to as the 'Hawthorne effect' following a series of studies in the 1920s at the Hawthorne Electrical Company in the US in which it appeared that the mere act of doing something with employees improved their productivity almost regardless of what it was that was done (Brown, 1954). The Hawthorne effect may not last all that long but it can be an unintended feature of the experimental programme that makes it appear successful. One solution is to provide the control group with something extra which, even if it does not include the key ingredient of parental involvement, is comparable in terms of extra attention and resources. For example, in the Haringey project Tizard *et al.* (1982) had comparison classes that received extra small-group teaching in school as well as comparison classes that had no extra provision. Another aspect of this problem is that the success of a parent involvement programme may depend upon the quality of previous teaching and home–school links. The poorer these are, the more likely it is that focusing on the teaching of reading and the involvement of parents will bring about improvements in children's reading. Therefore an important part of any evaluation is to specify the control conditions so that it is as clear as possible what scope there was for improvement. The value of a programme is relative to some alternative so an evaluation is incomplete if it does not clearly specify that alternative.

The nature of the programme itself also needs to be clearly identified for it may not be what it seems. This is an aspect of evaluation to be considered in more detail in the next chapter when we look at implementation processes but, for the moment, it is sufficient to recognize its implications in experimental and quasi-experimental designs. For example, a reading at home project may be implemented in part through home visiting by teachers or others. If the programme is successful it may be because of the parental involvement or the home visiting or some interaction between the two. If a paired reading programme appears to be effective one may ask whether the procedure was followed exactly or whether parents 'lapsed' into a less structured way of hearing reading in which case the ingredients in the programme making for its success are unclear. Sometimes innovative programmes are introduced into schools by outside agencies such as education psychological services, universities or research units in which case, one may wonder whether their success, if any, is due to the programme itself or to the role of the agency.

Sampling can affect the validity of some research designs. The most vulnerable is the one-group pre-test/post-test design. If the children for a programme are selected on the basis of poor performance on a pre-test and the same (or similar) test is used as the post-test there is a good chance that many will improve anyway due to the statistical effect known as 'regression to the mean'. This happens because the low pre-test scores are partly a reflection of test error and this is unlikely to affect low scorers to the same extent on a second occasion — on the post-test. In a true experimental design the regression to the mean effect does not threaten validity but in quasi-experimental designs it can sometimes cause difficulties depending on how children are allocated to groups. A more general difficulty with sampling arises if a programme is implemented in such a way that it is taken up by such an atypical sample of children or parents that it is difficult to generalize findings. An obvious example would be a programme only for parents who volunteer in response to a general invitation. Even if experimental and control groups were drawn from the same sample the programme is likely to have different effects with such families than with families who have to be carefully approached individually to participate.

Selective parental involvement programmes (e.g. those directed at failing readers) represent a different form of sampling to comprehensive programmes (for all children). This can have important consequences for evaluation if group measures are used (e.g. mean scores). Comprehensive programmes will tend to include families where a significant proportion of parents are already in-volved in their children's literacy development whereas selective programmes can be expected to have fewer such families. In comprehensive programmes the measurable effect of any additional parental involvement is likely to be diluted because the gains for the previously uninvolved families have to be 'shared' arithmetically amongst the whole group. Selective programmes are more likely to show group gains simply because mean scores are less likely to be depressed in this way.

Not all research designs require groups. In *intra-subject* or *single-subject* designs each child is studied as an individual (Hersen and Barlow, 1977). Detailed measures of reading performance are repeatedly taken throughout, as well as at the end of, a programme. These are usually based on a reading curriculum of some kind (e.g. accuracy in reading lists of words or texts of certain difficulty levels) rather than standardized tests. To meet the objection that children usually improve anyway over a period of time, a baseline level of progress is established by measuring reading for a period prior to the programme and there may also be post-intervention measures to see if progress is maintained or falls back towards the baseline level. Results can be displayed graphically to show changes for each child so that it is usually possible to tell at a glance how they have fared. This approach has been used in evaluating special techniques such as 'pause, prompt and praise'. It has the advantage of making use of data from small samples, it avoids problems of finding suitable controls, it also avoids the problems of reading tests (whether standardized or not) by focusing on measures of performance which relate closely to the programme objectives. On the other hand it can be difficult for outsiders not familiar with the particular curriculum to judge the effectiveness of a pro-gramme in terms they can understand. Also, this kind of evaluation can be very demanding in the time needed to collect data (particularly if it is done sensitively enough so that children and parents do not feel constantly under test) and the time needed to analyse and present it adequately.

Reporting of Test-based Evaluations

For a report of a test-based evaluation to be useful to the wider educational community there is certain information it should provide. Table 9.2 lists some

Table 9.2: *Some question to ask about test-based evaluations*

QUESTION	SPECIFIC ISSUES
Are reasons given for carrying out the evaluation?	
Is the programme of involvement adequately described?	Target group. Objectives. Duration. Method.
Are problems of using a test recognized and discussed?	Justification of choice of test. Performance/competence relation. Match between programme activity and test performance activity. Adequacy of test standardization.
What test data are used?	Raw scores or standardized? Post-test scores only? Pre-test/post-test gains?
To what are test scores or gain scores of children in programme compared? What is the research design?	No comparison. Standardization sample. Control group (experiment). Comparison group (quasi-experiment). Intra-subject comparison.
Are control or comparison conditions specified?	
Are test data reported in sufficient detail?	
Are appropriate analyses carried out?	
Are conclusions consistent with the validity of the research design and analysis?	Internal validity. External validity.

essentials — most of the issues discussed so far in this chapter — that should be included in addition to the general requirements for evaluation reports discussed in the previous chapter.

It is particularly important that a test-based evaluation report should recognize problematic aspects of using tests and therefore explain why a particular test was used, how children's performance on that test might indicate reading competence, how closely it matches what they do in the programme, and, if standardized scores or 'reading ages' are used, how well the test was standardized. The kinds of test measures used (raw scores, post-test scores, or pre-test/post-test gains) should be made clear.

Misleading Research Designs

This brief review of research design problems in test-based evaluation has shown many ways in which they can be flawed. By way of summary it may be helpful to consider two extreme possibilities of misleading designs: one that exaggerates effects and one that underestimates them.

A design that might mislead by exaggerating the effects of parental involvement could have the following features: a close match between the reading test performance and the programme activity; a tradition of parental exclusion in the school setting (so that any parental involvement is a big change); a school setting where children underachieve for other reasons (e.g. poor teaching, high staff turnover, lack of books); populations with low likelihood of pre-existing parental involvement (e.g. selected poor readers); short duration (maximizing the Hawthorne effect); selection by poor pre-test scores with the same test used as a post-test (maximizing regression to the mean effects).

A design that might mislead by making it unlikely that parental involvement effects could show through could have the following features: reading test performance quite unlike the programme activity; high levels of pre-existing parent involvement (leaving little scope for increase); good pre-existing literacy standards or generally high teaching standards in the school (leaving little scope for improvement); populations with relatively high levels of pre-existing parental involvement (e.g. in comprehensive programmes); long duration (eliminating the Hawthorne effect); and no pre-test selection of children.

Chapter 10

Evaluation by Participants

I argued in the last chapter that test-based evaluation of parental involvement is not as straightforward a method of finding out 'what works' as it may first appear. There are difficulties in finding appropriate reading tests and difficulties in devising valid experimental designs. These difficulties are not insuperable; if we find a good test, recognize the nature of the reading test performance it requires, and devise an appropriate comparison for children's test scores, we can certainly draw some conclusions about the effects of parental involvement in a given setting. This may still not be the best way of evaluating practice, however.

It is doubtful whether any form of experimental test-based evaluation should be the only way of evaluating parental involvement given our present level of knowledge and the present stage of development in practice in the field. The task of evaluating parental involvement — truly assessing its value — means finding out much more than can possibly be learnt from one decisive experiment, or a whole series of experiments, however brilliantly designed and carried out. The main reason for this is that in an experiment one can usually only investigate a very limited number of factors. For example, we might be interested in the effect of two forms of involvement, in comparison with one control condition, for two categories of children. This could be studied in a 3 × 2 factorial design — not unusual in psychological research but more complex than designs used to study parental involvement in the teaching of literacy. Even so, it does not match the complexity of the range of situations in schools where parental involvement might be tried. There are so many different forms of involvement that could be attempted. One has only to think of the possible combinations of features discussed in Chapter 2, under the headings of target group, objectives, duration and method in Table 2.1, to realize just how many there could be. Schools, and classes within schools, also vary enormously so that there are many possible control conditions to which involvement programmes might be compared. Other factors to be considered are pupil and parent characteristics, reading materials, and the kinds of outcomes to be measured. Faced with permutations of all these factors it is clear that life is just too short to carry out all the experiments necessary to know for certain what forms of involvement will have what effects in what kinds of schools. Without such certainty one has to fall back on judgments about similarities and differences between cases to estimate what can be expected in one case from findings in another.

Another limit to the knowledge that can be gained from experimentation is that not all outcomes of value in a programme are equally susceptible to measurement but, unless one can measure something, at least to the extent of saying whether it occurs or not, experimental investigation is irrelevant. A good example is the issue of children's enjoyment of reading. This is certainly something to be valued in itself, not just as a precondition for reading achievement, but it is very difficult, if not impossible to measure. Pumfrey (1985) reviewed fifteen British and American tests of children's attitudes to reading. Almost all are intended for children aged 8 years or older, that is, beyond the period of many parental involvement programmes. Many are open to criticism on the grounds that what is being tested is so obvious to children that they are likely to respond in a 'pleasing teacher' direction. Several of the more sophisticated tests remain at an early stage of development and provide potential for the future rather than tools for the present. The result is that there is probably no 'off the shelf' measure of attitudes to reading that is appropriate for test-based evaluation of parent involvement. If enjoyment of reading is a valued outcome it is more likely to be detected in the course of systematic observations over a period of time rather than by what can be gleaned from performance in a single artificial test situation.

Observing over a period of time — perhaps over the entire period of a programme — and observing test performance for a few minutes at the end of a programme represent sharply contrasting approaches to evaluation. Test-based evaluation misses so much. The meaning of the experience to the participants — parents, children and teachers — is ignored. To get at that may require ethnographic methods — sustained observation and interaction with participants, including interviewing, over weeks or months — to understand the programme from their different, and possibly conflicting, viewpoints.

Test-based evaluation by itself also overlooks the fine grain detail of how the programme was implemented and how it worked, or failed to work, in practice. It cannot answer such important practical questions as how many parents accepted the invitation to become involved or how many remained involved throughout the period of the programme. Yet these are all vital pieces of information for determining the value of a programme.

The purpose of this chapter is to set out an alternative to test-based evaluation, one that could be called 'evaluation by participants' since it draws upon teachers and parents for data, examines what they do (and do not do), takes their perspectives seriously, and is also more feasible for teachers to carry out for themselves. It means studying several, overlapping issues: take-up, dropout, participation, implementation, involvement processes, teachers' views, and parents' views. In principle this approach could complement test-based evaluation but in practice it is more likely to be a qualitative substitute for the quantitative approach.

Take-up

Take-up is a very important indicator of the value of any form of involvement. It refers to the proportion of parents accepting an invitation to participate in a programme. If the programme originates from outside a school (e.g. an LEA initiative aimed at a number of schools) then take-up can also refer to the proportions of schools or teachers willing to participate.

If take-up falls short of 100 per cent the value of a programme may be open to question. If it is a long way short then the programme's value is obviously going to be limited to those prepared to take it up and those whom it does not reach cannot benefit at all. Even if take-up is close to 100 per cent it is important to know why some individuals chose not to participate. Is it because the programme failed to meet their needs? Did they have particular difficulties that a modified programme could address?

Low take-up could be a fatal weakness in a programme, discouraging those who initiate it from carrying on with it or repeating it in the future, and discouraging others elsewhere from trying it. In such circumstances there might not be any point in taking the evaluation further. Even if it is regarded less seriously, low take-up has other implications, particularly if there is an experimental component in the evaluation. Should the programme children be considered to include those who did not take it up or just those who did? If the former then it will be necessary to collect data such as test scores for non-participants as well as participants because it could be said that the 'treatment' was applied to all (even if some did not respond). If the latter, there is a difficulty in finding suitable controls which ought, if there is to be a valid comparison, to consist only of those who were invited to participate in a programme, who accepted the invitation, yet for some reason did not participate.

High take-up means that a programme has passed its first test. People are prepared to give it a try.

Calculating the level of take-up is usually straightforward. One needs to know the number of individuals invited to participate (e.g. those receiving a letter or introductory visit) and the proportion actually taking up the invitation (e.g. by saying 'yes', or getting to the first stage of involvement). Sometimes the number invited may be unclear (e.g. when an invitation is extended to an entire community or neighbourhood to take part in a family literacy programme) in which case the evaluators' duty is to make a reasoned estimate of how many people or families could have taken part. Despite its simplicity, despite how much it reveals about the perceived value and feasibility of a programme for individuals, and despite its consequences for the rest of the evaluation, many evaluation reports do not include information about take-up.

Participation Rate

Families who take up the opportunity for involvement, and who do not drop out, will still vary in the degree to which they participate in a programme. For example, in a programme that involves parents in hearing children read at home, some families will do it almost daily; some will do it intermittently. In a school-based workshop some parents will attend almost every occasion; others less often. It is usually possible to keep records that will allow some measure of participation, for example, actual attendances as a percentage of the maximum possible. Such measures have several uses. They can show the variation between families in participation; they can allow us to investigate any relationship between participation level and outcome measures; and they can show how the participation of an entire group of families changes — declines or increases — over the period of a programme. All this can be helpful in determining the value of a programme. For example, in the Belfield Reading Project, an analysis of home reading cards showed how institutional changes could cause short term fluctuations in participation levels (Hannon *et al.*, 1985) and how the low participation of a small number of families could be explained in terms of particularly severe combinations of 'adverse factors' (Weinberger *et al.*, 1986).

Dropout

After a programme starts, it is usual for some participants to drop out. This can be for many reasons unconnected with the programme, including children leaving a school, families leaving a neighbourhood, ill health, or domestic changes of various kinds. Even in control groups there is usually attrition. Obviously, the longer the programme, the greater the dropout is likely to be. Sometimes, however, dropout does tell us something about a programme. The logic is similar to that applying to take-up: the dropout rate reflects the value of a programme (low dropout, high value; high dropout, low value) and it has consequences for the rest of the evaluation, particularly if that is test-based.

Recording dropout from a programme is not quite as straightforward as recording take-up. There needs to be some measure of an individual's participation but the nature of that measure will vary according to the programme. For example, in a school-based family reading group or reading workshop a record of attendance could be kept (discreetly, perhaps, so as not to put people off). In a reading at home programme there should be records of what and how often children take books home to read. During the programme a working definition of dropout could be agreed (e.g. three successive absences or no home reading for a month) or it could be left until the end of the programme when it becomes clear whether individuals have withdrawn from it temporarily or completely. In principle this is straightforward enough but in practice it does take some effort to monitor dropout. Resources — principally time — have to be allowed for the appropriate record keeping. The possibilities for self-deception are enormous given that anyone working hard to involve parents can be tempted to overlook signs that some are not responding at all. Instead, it is natural to focus attention on those who are getting involved for they are the ones who appear to value the programme most and with whom it is most rewarding to work. The others are out of sight but their lack of response is nonetheless significant from the point of view of establishing the overall value of a programme.

Implementation

An adequate evaluation of a programme must include some evidence that it was properly implemented. Clearly, if it was not implemented at all then there is nothing to evaluate; if it was only partially implemented, the evaluation has to explain why, and take that into account in considering outcomes. In practice, programmes are rarely implemented as planned even if no one drops out. Participation levels are part of the story but even if they are maintained at 100 per cent and there is zero dropout, there will be degrees of implementation and varying degrees of involvement amongst parents. Information is needed on this if outsiders are to judge what kind of intervention produces any outcomes reported later.

There are two other reasons why evaluation ought to be concerned with implementation. First, any report on a programme ought to contain sufficient detail for someone else, unfamiliar with it, and working in another situation, to try the same thing. After all, one of the reasons for carrying out an evaluation and reporting findings is to share ideas amongst the educational community so that workers in different situations can build on each others' efforts and lessons learnt in one place can be applied in another. This is not possible unless what is done in a programme is described clearly and fully enough for it to be replicated. Second, there are usually unforeseen aspects of an implementation — unexpected problems, creative solutions to difficulties, or interesting issues thrown up — that are worth studying for the sake of a more complete understanding of what it is to involve parents. For example, a reading at home programme may have knock-on effects on classroom organization or a reading workshop may require excessive preparation time. If these issues can be identified in an evaluation, teachers elsewhere can be better prepared for dealing with the same thing themselves.

Some examples may help. One form of involvement in which implementation has been very carefully studied is 'pause, prompt and praise'. In this procedure it is important that parents delay attending to pupil errors, that they prompt (rather than supply the correct word), and that they provide plenty of praise. To confirm that this is indeed happening a number of studies have made audiotape recordings of reading sessions and have analysed the parent–child interaction (Glynn and McNaughton, 1985). Implementation of the Belfield Reading Project was studied in several ways. The approach to parents was described in an initial report (Jackson and Hannon, 1981). Data on the frequency of home reading sessions from home–school reading cards was analysed, parents and teachers were interviewed about what they had done, and

Figure 10.1: Involvement processes

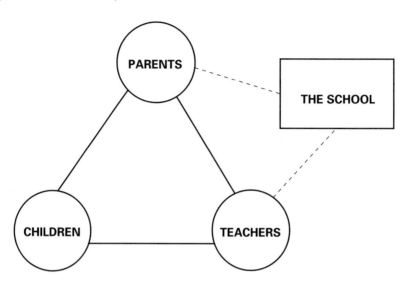

parent–child interaction was studied through audiotapes of reading sessions (Hannon and Jackson, 1987b). In the Fox Hill Reading Workshop implementation was checked by analysis of attendance records and the workshops activities were described in considerable detail (Weinberger, 1983). In paired reading, some studies have investigated whether parents actually do hear children read in the prescribed manner (Toepritz, 1982; Wareing, 1985; Winter, 1990).

An example of how *not* to report implementation is provided by Widlake and Macleod (1984). They conducted a test-based evaluation of the Coventry Community Education Project — admittedly a difficult task given that it included several schools — but reported the implementation of the programme by providing 'accounts' of some activities which they hoped would be 'sufficient to give the reader the "feel" of the parental involvement' (p.8). The accounts are interesting but it is quite impossible to tell precisely what was done, with how many parents and children, over what length of time. The result is that workers elsewhere seeking to do the same research cannot tell whether they are implementing the same programme or indeed whether the Coventry programme is something they might have already tried.

Involvement Processes

Once a programme is underway it can be viewed as a set of interrelated processes. Figure 10.1 illustrates this schematically. First, within the circles, *individuals* are likely to change during a programme. We hope that children will become better readers or writers (in terms of their enjoyment and use of literacy as well as their competence at it) but they may change in other ways too, such as their self-confidence, classroom behaviour, or choice of home leisure activities. There may be changes in *parents'* confidence and competence as teachers of their own children, their interest in children's literacy and learning, or in their own literacy. Changes in *teachers* could relate to their awareness of children's home environments, teaching methods, attitudes to parents, or general professional development. Changes in individuals can be understood as processes in the sense that they are not sudden and inexplicable occurrences but gradual developments arising from a set of experiences and the interplay of discernible factors.

Second, there is *interaction between individual*, represented in Figure 10.1 by lines connecting circles. *Teacher–parent* interaction is crucial in getting the parental involvement started and then maintaining it. There are many important processes here that can be grouped under the general heading of 'home–school communication' and that include teachers talking to parents informally or in parent evenings, home visiting, meetings in school, letters and circulars, or two-way use of reading cards. At the heart of any involvement programme, however, is the *parent–child* interaction and no evaluation is complete which treats what happens here uncritically. It might include the process of hearing children read (whether that is done according to some prescription or as the parent chooses), the implicit messages parents convey to children about reading and schools, the structuring of involvement activities in the busy round of family life, and also what children bring to the interaction in terms of their enthusiasm and enjoyment. The third side of the triangle is completed by *child–teacher* interaction which is a part of any involvement programme as well as being a central process of school life. Processes of interest here include how teachers treat children's home learning (whether they ignore it or show children that they respect it), how their relationship with children alters, and how children respond to them in the context of a closer home–school relationship.

There can be important interactions outside the basic triangle, principally those concerning the school as a whole, that may undergo change because of a parental involvement programme. Both parents and teachers can have an impact on the school as suggested in Figure 10.1. For example, as a result of their experience in a programme, teachers may seek changes such as re-ordered INSET priorities for the school, better arrangements for parents' evenings or a change in language policy. Parents may develop new attitudes towards school that lead to them standing as parent governors, setting up a bookshop or to question as existing language policy. It may not have been the intention of the programme to produce changes at the level of the school but if such processes occur then they can be a legitimate concern of an evaluation.

Why should such processes be studied in an evaluation, however? There are at least three good reasons. First, they can be interesting in their own right and deserving of study if we are to improve general understanding of the education of young children. An involvement programme can open up opportunities for research (e.g. to study parent–child interaction at home) which are otherwise quite rare. Second, a close look at processes can reveal the deep structure of involvement — the many fundamental, yet subtle, ways in which involvement can be realized and flourish or the ways in which it can be subverted and choked. Aspects of involvement which on the surface appear to be working well or working badly can mean something different when the underlying significance is probed more deeply. Third, it is possible, having identified and studied particular processes, to reach some conclusions about their value. That is, we can judge whether what is happening is congruent with the aims of a programme or our wider educational values. For example, if a close study of home–school communication processes reveals that teachers initiate most exchanges, or that a significant number of parents do not communicate anything at all, it is reasonable to conclude that this aspect of the programme is not as valuable as we would wish. If a study of parent–child interaction in a school-based reading workshop shows parents using school resources imaginatively in ways that had not occurred to teachers then, without too much deliberation, we ought to be able to say that this is of value. The justification for such value judgments is not usually to be found in experimental proof that one way of doing things is better than another but in the professional judgment of quality based on some kind of defensible educational theory.

The next question is to consider *how* such processes can be studied. There are no hard and fast rules. Different processes demand different methods and much depends on the resources and creativity of the evaluator. Obviously, one cannot expect to study all processes at once in one evaluation; a decision has to be made about which ones matter from the point of view of developing future practice. In the case of processes that have to be studied anyway as part of checking of implementation it may only be a question of taking things a little further. For example, in the Belfield Project, weekly reading cards were collected and analysed to see how often parents recorded that their children had read to them at home. This provided a useful measure of implementation but the cards were also for teachers and parents to write comments to each other so there was an opportunity to see how an unusual, written, form of home–school communication had developed (Hannon *et al.*, 1986b). It emerged that many comments were simply 'procedural', concerned with what had been read; others were 'evaluative', exchanging information on how well children had read; and some were 'teaching' comments concerned with children's specific difficulties or successes or techniques to help them. The evaluation found that the cards were very valuable for some parents and teachers but more could be done in the future to show all parents and teachers their potential. Another form of home–school communication in the Belfield Project was home visiting — an approach that, as the project continued, seemed quite important so an attempt was made to evaluate it directly using interview data and the visitor's notes (Hannon and Jackson, 1987b). The same project also provided an opportunity to study parent–child interaction in home reading sessions. As described in Chapter 6, analysis of audio recordings of parents (and teachers) hearing children read showed not just that parents were performing competently in that role, but that there were specific aspects of their strategies that the adults could probably improve (Hannon *et al.*, 1986a). These examples demonstrate that the range of methods used to study involvement processes can extend over the whole range of qualitative and quantitative methods used in educational and psychological research.

Teachers' views

Teachers' views about work with parents are usually decisive so it would be a serious mistake to leave this aspect out of any evaluation or even to subordinate it to supposedly 'harder' test data. If teachers find involvement stimulating and rewarding and if *they* think it benefits children then they will continue it, develop it and share their ideas with colleagues elsewhere. On the other hand, if their experience is disappointing the most highly significant test results are unlikely to convince them of the value of carrying on.

There are several ways in which teachers' views can be obtained. They can produce them themselves either in written form — notes, jottings, considered reflections, journals — or by audiotape recordings. The latter technique can be useful if there is a group of teachers working together; a group discussion can be recorded and transcribed or main points and quotations abstracted for a report. Interviewing of one another or by an outsider are other possibilities. The right kind of outsider — interested, sympathetic, but sceptical — can pose the questions that are most likely to be in the minds of others interested in a programme's value. If possible it is much better to collect teachers' views during the project — indeed right from the beginning — rather than just at the end. Changes in views, as well as the final view, are needed. As in other parts of an evaluation study, this can take time and if it is to be done properly the time and other resources required need to be allowed for in advance.

Teachers' views can provide a damning verdict on a programme or a powerful endorsement of it. To take another example from the Belfield Project, one teacher told an interviewer at the end, 'Without a doubt it's improved [children's] ability to read and their liking for it' and another said, 'I'd always like to teach reading this way' (Hannon, 1986). Such very positive comments from experienced teachers deserve serious attention. Nevertheless it is surprising that teachers' views do not figure very prominently in the literature.

One problem is that such views do need to be treated *critically*. It can be argued that teachers who have worked on a programme, whatever their professional competence and personal honesty, are not well placed to provide the best view of its value. There are two ways of dealing with this problem. First, no evaluation should rely solely on teachers' views. Other data, including all the points discussed so far, and parents' views, to be discussed below, should be set alongside what teachers say. If they point to the same conclusion, fine; if not, an attempt must be made to reconcile conflicting evidence. This approach has been called 'triangulation' — getting a more accurate measure of something by viewing it from two or more perspectives. Second, one can also treat teachers' views critically, and respectfully, by examining the internal logic. If teachers claim that children's reading has improved, what grounds do they have for saying so? What is understood by 'children's reading'? Were they ready to look for signs of failure as well as success? Would it have been difficult for them to accept that the programme had not improved reading? Has classroom teaching been modified to take account of better reading? In asking teachers for their views (or when they ask themselves what they think) it is important to establish a climate in which both positive and negative views are acceptable. Expressing a negative view of a programme (e.g. that it took too much time) can be a very positive response if it is well-founded. It does not necessarily mean the end of parental involvement; it could lead to a more efficient way of achieving it. Negative feedback in an evaluation, whether from implementation findings or participants' views, is not a disaster to be feared but helpful information that may lead to better ways of doing things in the future.

Parents' Views

The importance of parents' views is obvious. The whole point of a programme is to gain their active, positive involvement in children's literacy development. An evaluation therefore has to include asking parents whether they have been active, how they have been active and what positive and negative views they have about the experience. As in the case of teachers, negative views are not fatal but formative. Parents are also well placed to tell us about children's views, which are difficult to discover directly.

The best method for studying parents' views is probably through structured interviewing, preferably by an outsider. Teachers themselves could interview the parents with whom they have been working but an independent interviewer is more likely to elicit both negative and positive views since these inevitably touch on how well the teachers have done their job. An outsider could be a teacher colleague from another school (who might receive similar assistance in evaluation in return). The structure of the interview — the main points on which information is sought — should be agreed with those who initiated and implemented the programme. Parents could be guaranteed anonymity but not confidentiality, that is, their views will be passed on but not their identity except in so far as it can be inferred from their views. If there are not enough resources (particularly time) to interview all parents in a programme then a representative sample could be selected. Probably the best way to do this is by picking names at random, for example, names out of a hat, or every fifth name from an alphabetical list. The point is to avoid unwittingly choosing a biased sample, such as those parents who have most contact with teachers. It must be acknowledged that this aspect of evaluation can be very time consuming if it has to include the construction of an interview schedule, arranging interviews, interviewing, transcribing some or all of the interviews (if they were recorded), producing transcripts or full notes, collating responses to key questions, analysing responses, and writing up the analysis. However, it is so crucial a source of information, likely to be so helpful to teachers, that some attempt should be made to interview at least a few parents. If some or all the parents cannot be interviewed then a questionnaire survey could be considered. At least one study has found this to be practicable (Ashton *et al.*, 1986). The main problems to be overcome in a questionnaire survey are devising and trialling the questions and sending out reminders to obtain the best possible response rate.

It is important to treat parents' views just as critically as those of teachers, but it is more difficult because it is not reasonable to question parents as intently as one might question teachers. Ways can still be found to explore why parents hold certain views through gentle prompts and questions. Most parents, most of the time, are appreciative of teachers' efforts to help their children, particularly in the early primary years. They may well appreciate the fact of teachers trying to make some effort to involve them even if what is done is less than ideal. Consequently, negative views can be difficult to elicit. An interview schedule or questionnaire should make it easy for parents to express criticisms in a non-damaging way. It may be easier, for example, if the questions come from some independent person not seen to be part of the programme (e.g. in the evaluation of the Sheffield Early Literacy Development Project by Hannon *et al.*, 1991). Also, instead of simply asking, 'Did you find this kind of involvement valuable?' one might ask, 'Can you suggest how it could be improved?' In the Belfield evaluation, to make it easy for them to express reservations, parents were asked whether they thought too much had been asked of them and whether they would like to carry on for a further year (Hannon, 1986). It actually proved rather difficult to elicit any negative views, and, although this tells us something about the value of the programme, it does point to a methodological problem. It may be that parents will welcome almost anything schools do to involve them in which case their views may not help us decide between the merits of different forms of involvement. However, it is still worth trying to obtain their views because, if parental involvement becomes more common, parents may become more discerning. Their views may become increasingly helpful in shaping practice in the future. In the meantime there is no harm in teachers receiving some encouragement in their work, and they stand to gain quite a lot from parents.

Chapter 11

What Have We Learned?
What Do We Need to Know?

In this concluding chapter I want to assess what we have learned from research into parental involvement in the teaching of literacy over the past decade or so. Often this means trying to make use of evaluations which have flawed designs or are poorly reported. Where possible I have drawn on other researchers' reviews or discussions of the issues (Leler, 1983; Becher, 1985; Glynn and McNaughton, 1985; Pumfrey, 1986; Swinson, 1986; Miller, 1987; Vinograd-Bausell and Bausell, 1987; Drummond *et al.*, 1990; Topping and Lindsay, 1992; Toomey, 1993). My aim is to examine findings in relation to certain key issues. I then want to go on to identify five broad research questions which I urge as a research agenda for the years to come.

What We Have Learned

The issues I propose to examine are: open approaches to parents hearing children read; prescriptive approaches to hearing reading; the relative merits of open and proscriptive approaches; behaviourist approaches; in-school involvement; preschool work with parents; and family literacy.

Open Approaches to Parents Hearing Children Read

In the Haringey Project, the first major initiative to change home–school relations in the teaching of literacy, Tizard *et al.* (1982) found that a fairly open approach to parents hearing children read produced educationally significant gains. The approach was widely taken up in British schools and several cases have been documented or evaluated. Toomey (1993) lists four studies (Friend, 1983; Ashton *et al.*, 1986; Bloom, 1987; Hannon, 1987) and, pointing out that none of them succeeded in replicating the Haringey effects, he concludes that this approach is relatively ineffective. However, the studies by Bloom and Friend can be discounted because of vague reporting and too many differences between experimental and control/comparison groups. That leaves two studies whose findings conflict with Haringey. Against this there are at least eight other studies which, like Haringey, have found gains (David, 1983; Dyson and Swinson, 1982; Crawford, 1983; Bartlett *et al.*, 1984; Lindsay *et al*, 1985; Webb *et al.*, 1985; Burdett, 1986; Leach and Siddall, 1990). Individually some of these studies have design weaknesses (in no case, I think, fatal) but collectively they all tell the same story — open approaches to hearing reading can produce gains. Also, the Hannon (1987) and Ashton *et al.* (1986) studies did report some gains although too small to be statistically significant. Therefore there is no justification for concluding that such approaches are ineffective.

The problem here is to explain why open approaches sometimes produce gains and sometimes do not. It is interesting to note that the eight studies that found gains were all of short duration — weeks rather than months or years. I argue later that almost any approach has a positive effect *if it is of short duration*. The programmes evaluated by Hannon (1987) and Ashton *et al.* (1986) were three years and one year respectively. It is possible that if reading tests had been administered after children had been in the programmes only a few weeks, they might have revealed gains similar to those found in short duration programmes. There still remains the fact that the two-year Haringey programme resulted in more substantial gains than any other study has found. I have suggested previously (Hannon, 1987) that three features of the Haringey Project might explain the difference: well-resourced and structured home visits, low levels of pre-existing parental involvement, and more families for whom English was a second language.

The sensible thing to do at this point would be to run further experiments to test out some of the hypotheses I have put forward to account for conflicting findings. That this has not happened is a reflection of the difficulty of conducting field experiments or quasi-experiments in schools and the lack of resources available for such research. Meanwhile the implication for practice would seem to be that open approaches to parents hearing reading should be continued. Short duration programmes tend to produce measurable gains and longer ones can do too — under circumstances that are not yet well understood. It is also important to remember that reading test gains are not the only outcome to be valued and, time and again, studies have reported a very positive — often enthusiastic — response by parents, children and teachers to involvement programmes.

Prescriptive Approaches to Parents Hearing Children Read

There have been many evaluations of the most common prescriptive approach, paired reading, but again the quality is very variable with a heavy reliance on one-group pre-test/post-test designs or weak comparison designs. Topping and Lindsay (1992) have produced an extremely valuable and detailed review of forty studies and have also reported details of numerous other programmes provided for over 1700 children in the Kirklees Project. Programmes tend to be of short duration (typically between six and ten weeks), selective, for failing readers, and mostly evaluated by individual oral reading tests. It is quite clear overall that such programmes do produce gains in reading test scores, typically increasing 'reading ages' by three or four or more months (above what might have been expected anyway over the duration of a programme) and that gains are maintained, or even increased a little, for a time afterwards. It is difficult to draw any further conclusions from such a shaky and heterogeneous set of studies but that should not detract from the importance of the overall finding — that this particular prescriptive approach definitely 'works' in the sense of improving reading test performance.

Paired reading is not the only prescriptive approach to produce gains. Greening and Spencely (1987) found that the simpler 'shared reading' approach produced gains. A review of eight well-designed and well-reported studies of 'pause, prompt and praise' parent involvement programmes by Glynn and McNaughton (1985) showed consistent positive effects. Leach and Siddall (1990) found both paired reading and pause, prompt and praise produced gains. There is also evidence that other prescriptive approaches described in Chapter 7 are effective (Bryans *et al.*, 1985; Young and Tyre, 1983).

All the prescriptive approaches therefore seem to produce gains but, as the evidence comes from evaluations of short duration programmes, it is not known whether long duration programmes comparable to those in which open approaches have been tried would be feasible or effective.

Comparison of Open and Prescriptive Approaches

The obvious question to ask is whether some approaches to parents hearing reading are better than others. Are prescriptive approaches better than open ones? Are some prescriptive approaches better than others? It would be easy to answer if some never produced gains while others did not but, as they all seem to produce gains to some degree in short duration programmes, the question poses certain difficulties.

One difficulty in making comparisons is being sure that particular approaches are actually implemented. For example, several studies of *involvement processes* in paired reading suggest that, in practice, some parents deviate from the prescribed approach and lapse into strategies close to those found in open approaches (Toepritz, 1982; Wareing, 1985; Winter, 1990). Therefore, if there are differences between approaches, it may not be due to what parents actually do with their children so much as to other features such as how a technique is commonly presented to parents or to what extent benefits are promised. It can be difficult to decide which features of an approach are unique and which could be applied to any. For example, if some approaches are usually introduced to parents by demonstration or if they are supported by regular home visits they may be more effective for that reason alone.

The basic difficulty is how to compare like with like. If approaches are to be compared they have to be tried within programmes that are comparable in terms of ages of children, selectivity, the pre-existing levels of reading attainment and parental involvement, duration, and, if tests are used, similarity of test performance requirements. Otherwise any differences that result might only be a reflection of features of the programme or the evaluation rather than of the approaches in question. Particularly misleading is any attempt to compare comprehensive strategies (where the impact on previously non-involved parents is diluted by the presence of parents who are already involved) with selective programmes (where a higher proportion of parents are likely to be affected).

There have been three studies in which approaches have been compared under reasonably well controlled conditions. Lindsay *et al.* (1985) found no difference between paired reading and an open approach (which they termed 'relaxed reading') for older failing readers. Burdett (1986) also reported no difference between paired reading and an open approach in terms of test scores. Leach and Siddall (1990) found 'paired reading' and 'pause, prompt and praise' somewhat superior to a (relatively unsupported) open approach for young middle-ability children but even there a confounding variable was the amount of training and support provided with each approach. Topping and Lindsay (1992) cite five further studies, two of which found paired reading superior to an open approach and three of which found no difference. There are no reports of open approaches being superior to paired reading. Overall, then, paired reading prescriptive approach is either only marginally better than an open approach or just as effective as an open approach.

We need to keep a sense of perspective in comparing approaches. It is tempting for inventors or advocates of particular approaches to try to show the superiority of their product over others (e.g. Topping, 1986) but this is not the most helpful way forward for two reasons.

First, as a number of writers have pointed out, it is more important to try to work out the strengths and weaknesses of the various approaches in order to find out why they have the effects they do and in what circumstances they might be most useful (Drummond *et al.*, 1990; Miller, 1987; Swinson, 1986; Pumfrey, 1986; Pumfrey, 1986; Hewison, 1988; Leach and Siddall, 1990). In relation to paired reading, for example, Miller (1987) has suggested that it may be particularly appropriate for poorly motivated, failing readers when parents or teachers are unsure about parental involvement and the parent finds it difficult to check negative reactions. In relation to 'pause, prompt and praise', Leach and Siddall (1990) have suggested that it might be preferred after the early stages of reading and in situations where a programme could be maintained for several months. In the case of the open approach, I would argue that it should be considered as a basic form of involvement in the early school years, provided that parents are supported in reflecting on their role (as suggested in Chapter 6) and that it is supplemented from time to time with other approaches if children are not progressing. Table 11.1 lists approaches in the order in which they might be considered.

Table 11.1:   Choosing approaches to parents hearing reading: Some suggestions

Situation	Possible approach	Relevant studies
Young children not yet reading any text independently.	Shared storybook reading with adult allowing children to take over as much of the shared task as they are able.	Hannon *et al.* (1991)
All children in a 'reading aloud' stage of reading development	'Open' approach (with some support for parents to think about their strategies).	Tizard *et al.* (1982) Hannon *et al.* (1986a) Hannon (1987)
As a variant on the above, or as the first recourse for children experiencing difficulties	'Shared reading'	Greening and Spencely (1987)
For children or parents experiencing difficulties; for teachers and parents uneasy about parental involvement	'Paired reading'	Miller *et al.* (1986) Topping and Lindsay (1992)
As above, but in situations where there are time and resources for a longer programme, training and monitoring.	'Pause, prompt and praise'	Glynn and McNaughton (1985)
As a last resort.	Direct instruction or behaviourist approaches (in. parallel with meaningful literacy activities)	Leach and Siddall (1990)

Second, it keeps matters in perspective to recognize that there is no evidence that any of the available approaches are so effective as to overcome the inequalities of literacy discussed in Chapter 1. Variations in literacy attainment (e.g. between social classes) were discussed there in terms of *years* of development whereas, at best, the approaches reviewed here produce gains of the order of *months*.

Behaviourist Approaches

There is evidence that behaviourist parental involvement programmes work in that children do learn what the programmes set out to teach (Leler, 1983; White *et al.*, 1984; Becher, 1985; Vinograd-Bausell and Bausell, 1987; Leach and Siddall, 1990). In the Leach and Siddall (1990) study the gains made on a parent involvement direct instruction programme also showed up in childrens' performance on an individual oral reading test.

In-school Involvement

There appears to have been very little systematic evaluation of these forms of involvement. The Coventry Community Education Project as described by

Widlake and Macleod (1984) was a major initiative which included a number of parental involvement literacy-focused activities in schools but lack of implementation measures and weak research design (problems discussed in Chapters 9 and 10) make it impossible to draw conclusions about effectiveness.

Preschool Work with Parents

The forms of school-age involvement reviewed so far are certainly helpful but, considered as a whole, they are rather limited. They focus on one aspect of literacy — reading — to the neglect of writing. Even the concern with reading is limited to a rather narrow concentration on oral reading of books to adults — clearly an important experience during one stage of early reading development but only relevant for a period as short as a year or two for many children. They also concentrate on the period after school entry but, as argued in Chapters 3 and 4, much literacy development takes place before school. We need a broader conception of literacy and one that acknowledges the importance of the preschool period. This reasoning led me in the late 1980s to research into preschool work with parents which tried to encompass the whole range of literacy experiences, including, for example, early writing/mark making and encounters with environmental print (Hannon, 1990).

The literature on preschool programmes, discussed in Chapter 4, shows that many forms of preschool involvement are possible but, apart from the Sheffield Early Literacy Development Project (Hannon *et al.*, 1991) most studies have concentrated on parent–child book sharing and increasing opportunities for this rather than other aspects of the parent's role. Several studies, using reasonably good evaluation designs, have reported measurable benefits (Swinson, 1985; Griffiths and Edmonds, 1986; McCormick and Mason, 1986). Limitations on this research include the lack of good measures of early literacy development (Nutbrown and Hannon, 1993) and follow-up studies to determine whether preschool intervention with parents produces benefits in terms of later school literacy attainment. Preschool involvement is not as well tried as school-age involvement but it deserves continued development and evaluation.

Family Literacy

There are two questions to be asked about the effectiveness of family literacy (understood here as combined programmes to raise parents' and children's literacy at the same time as getting parents to help their children). First, do children and parents benefit? Second, more important, do they benefit more than if they were in other kinds of programmes? For both questions, research is lacking. Nickse (1993) has commented, 'there is but modest evidence to date that family and intergenerational literacy programmes work' (p.34).

On the first question, there is some evidence that in the Kenan model both parents and children benefit (Seaman *et al.*, 1991; Darling and Hayes, n.d.) but given its very intensive and sustained nature it would be very surprising if there were not benefits. Nurss (1993) however has reported evaluations of three programmes where benefits to children were not matched by benefits to parents. A problem in such programmes, and in evaluating them, is participation and dropout. Interim findings from the national (US) evaluation of the Even Start programme indicate gains in family literacy type programmes for both parents and children of the order of what might be expected in conventional adult-only or child-only programmes (St. Pierre *et al.*, 1993).

The second question is harder to answer but, in the long run, more important. Determining whether family literacy is better than the alternatives depends on identifying the alternatives to which it ought to be compared. It is not really surprising that family literacy is better than nothing at all (although it would helpful to have proper experimental evidence to indicate how much better). But is a family literacy programme better for parents than, say, any good quality adult literacy and basic education responsive to the needs of learners (who often include undereducated, unemployed, unconfident mothers)? Is it better for children than good quality early education provision that has a concern for children's literacy development and that values the involvement of parents (including those with literacy difficulties)? Answers to these questions are needed to guide future policy for, if family literacy proves to be more effective in cost-benefit terms than other programmes then, depending on how much better it is, there could be far reaching implications for the organization of both early childhood and adult education. Research is lacking on these questions but future reports promised from the US national Even Start evaluation and the National Centre for Family Literacy may shed light on them.

What We Need to Know

Research has brought us a long way in understanding the home–school dimension in the teaching of literacy but it has also highlighted new questions that now need to be researched. I suggest five broad issues that might constitute a research agenda for the years to come:

1 effects of different forms of involvement;
2 effects of combining different forms of involvement;
3 unexplored areas;
4 support and training for teachers;
5 definition and position of school literacy.

Effects of different Forms of Involvement

There is a continued need to assess the effects of all forms of involvement. Most work has been done in relation to parents hearing children read and has shown that open and prescriptive approaches usually produce gains, at least in short duration programmes. There need to be more studies of long duration programmes and more well-controlled studies comparing different approaches, in both short duration and long duration programmes with children of different ages and reading abilities. In general, the quality of evaluations and reporting needs to be raised, in line with the suggestions of Chapters 8, 9 and 10. In the future it would be preferable to have fewer studies conducted at a higher standard rather than the huge number we have had in recent years conducted at a rather low standard. Research should not be confined to outcomes — whether determined by tests or by participants — but should also evaluate the crucial issues of take-up, participation and dropout, implementation and the quality of involvement processes.

Hearing children read at home is only one form of parental involvement in the teaching of literacy. Others, directed at different aspects of reading, at writing, and at preschool development (see Chapter 4) also need to be developed and compared systematically to control conditions and alternative approaches.

Effects of Combining Different Forms of Involvement

Having established that various forms of involvement have positive effects the next, and more exciting, phase of development and research should ask, 'What happens when different forms of involvement are combined, either simultaneously or sequentially?' For example, if a basic open approach to parents hearing reading is maintained over, say, a two year period, what extra benefits accrue from adding on short bursts of, say, pause, prompt and praise or a writing at home programme or a family reading group? If preschool involvement has benefits can they be increased by a carrying on with a different kind of programme after school entry? What does an adult literacy programme for parents add to the effects of programmes directed at children? Many permutations are possible. The key question is whether the effects are additive or are subject to diminishing returns. It is probable that they will be additive in so far as different forms of involvement focus on different aspects of children's home literacy. However, this is a question to be settled empirically.

Unexplored Areas

Any overview of parental involvement in the teaching of literacy reveals huge uncharted areas. The biggest is *writing* which, in developmental terms, is inextricably linked to reading development. Yet in terms of parental involvement practice, it has generally been ignored. Studies by Green (1987) and Hannon *et al.* (1991) indicate some paths that might be followed but progress in this area probably requires better analyses of pre-existing patterns of writing in families than are currently available in the research literature.

Another unexplored area, despite the studies cited in Chapter 4, is *pre-school education*. There has been a concentration on increasing children's opportunities for book sharing (without always influencing interaction) but little attention to the many other aspects of literacy known to be developing before children reach school. Also unexplored is *secondary education*. There have been attempts to develop or extend some forms of involvement in secondary teaching through parents hearing pupils read in an open approach (Ebbutt and Barber, 1978) or a prescriptive — paired reading — approach (Spalding *et al.*, 1984) but these have been restricted to failing readers at the start of secondary education. Beverton *et al.* (1993) refer to a family reading group in a secondary school. There are probably other, undocumented initiatives but in general there is nothing to match the shift in practice that has taken place in primary schools. Clearly, there are very different, and probably fewer, possibilities for work with parents of older children but, given that reading outside school is strongly associated with attainment in secondary education (Applebee *et al.*, 1988), there must be some scope for collaboration with parents.

The *family dimension* in parental involvement needs closer study. There is the issue of which members of the family are affected or involved by involvement programmes. Too often in practice, for example, 'parent' means 'mother'. The implications of this for the meaning of parental involvement have not been explored. To what extent do involvement programmes add to women's responsibilities or confirm their child-centred role in families? What messages about gendered aspects of literacy are being conveyed to children? What can be done to involve fathers? Is it better to continue using the word 'parent' to acknowledge the fact that fathers ought to be involved, and that some always are, or should 'mother' be used, at the risk of reinforcing stereotypes, because it is a more honest description of the reality of many programmes? Apart from the relative contributions of fathers and mothers, there are brothers, sisters, grandparents, aunts, uncles and others in many families. What is their role, and can schools collaborate in any way with them in children's interests? In addition to the literacy system within the family, there is the question of what literacy the various members bring into the family from the community or workplace. Research into these questions could provide a firmer base for school-initiated involvement initiatives.

Research into *involvement processes* has been neglected in favour of an emphasis on outcomes but, as argued in Chapter 10, a close observation of what happens within and between children, parents, teachers and schools can in itself be a guide to the value of a programme. A key area is parent–child interaction in shared reading episodes. The parent's strategies in hearing children read from storybooks is perhaps the most important aspect (Chapter 6) but in the preschool and later school periods other aspects of text-based interaction can be a focus for intervention and therefore for research too. Other processes might relate to parent–teacher communication or — in as yet undeveloped forms of involvement — to writing activities.

Intrinsic to all forms of parental involvement is *home–school communication* but how various channels of communication are used, and to what effect, remains underresearched. The channels available to parents and schools include written messages (circulars, notes, reading cards, posters), individual face to face meetings (parents' evenings, home visits, informal encounters), telephone calls (probably an underused channel), group meetings (large, small, workshops), videos (school-produced, off-air TV recordings, training videos), and the children themselves who constantly cross and recross the home–school boundary with information about one world for the other. Inadequate communication can be fatal to parental involvement; good communication can make it vital and responsive to developments as they occur. Where parents have literacy difficulties themselves, the importance and difficulty of home–school communication is even greater (Weinberg, 1990). Of interest here, from a research point of view, is what might be called the *deep structure of communication.* On the surface, home–school communication may seem to encourage parental involvement but what is communicated at a deeper level can be more powerful, and in conflict with the surface message. For example, at a surface level parents may be told at a meeting that they are their child's most important teacher but if at the same time the only views heard about how and what children should be taught come from the school staff, the parents may register at a deeper level that they are not all *that* important. Some studies have been carried out into home visiting (Hannon and Jackson, 1987a) and into the use of reading cards (Hannon *et al.*, 1986b) but further progress probably requires some kind of independent ethnographic research.

Support and Training for Teachers

School teachers, certainly in Britain, are poorly trained and supported for work with parents. It ·is often overlooked or given scant attention in initial training (Atkin and Bastiani, 1988) and does not get high priority in in-service training. There is a need for development and research in both contexts. Hannon and Welch (1993) have described and evaluated a research-based workshop initiative to give secondary trainee teachers an opportunity to learn about parents' perspectives directly by interviewing parents. This approach might be adapted for teachers of other age groups and given more of a literacy emphasis. Nutbrown, Hannon and Weinberger (1991) have argued for the key role of post-experience training when teachers know more about children's learning and may be better prepared personally to work with parents.

Definition and Position of School Literacy

It was argued in Chapter 1 that school literacy is a social construction and that the activities and abilities that are emphasized within it may differ from the literacies of family, community or workplace. From this point of view parental involvement in the teaching of literacy means enlisting parents' support in promoting a literacy for their children that may not be the one they have themselves, either at home or in the community or at work. We need to understand this better if we are to be fully aware of what we are doing in developing parental involvement.

Those of us who value parental involvement in the teaching of literacy face a dilemma. On the one hand we wish to listen to learn from parents, to respect their language and literacy, and we do not want uncritically to impose school literacy on families. On the other hand, school literacy is our business and it is self-deceiving to imagine that involvement can mean wholly accepting all families' literacies as a substitute for school literacy. For many families, involvement in the teaching of literacy is bound to mean being involved in new and different forms of literacy.

For example, the narrative fiction genre figures very prominently in texts used in the early years in school but, as Heath (1982) has so clearly shown, some families do not habitually use written language in this way. Other examples might be essay writing, poetry, reading nineteenth-century fiction. Promoting school literacy in such families runs the risk of importing — maybe even subtly *imposing* — new uses for written language without changing the cultural context that supports the existing uses. Yet, not to do anything or simply reflecting back and facilitating the family's existing uses for literacy may simply reinforce children's exclusion from school and whatever benefits school success confers.

How can research help? It can begin to chart the exact nature of school and family literacies in specific school contexts. Specific information, rather than generalities, may help us understand in what ways the two literacies are congruent or divergent, and the nature of parents' aspirations. All social action involves dilemmas but it is better to be aware of their nature than have them hidden. Working at the home–school literacy boundary is both rewarding and uncomfortable since it means having a critical awareness of two worlds of literacy, both of which have value but neither of which can be accepted wholly or uncritically. Research findings by themselves will not resolve the dilemma of whose literacy we are to promote but research may bring the issues into sharper focus and provide us with concepts for thinking out courses of action and with a vocabulary for dialogue with parents.

Conclusion

Since the early 1980s there has been a very significant change in educators' thinking about literacy at home and in school, and of the role of parents in the teaching of literacy. It is now almost inconceivable that there could be a return to school-centred views of literacy as something children only learn as a result of being taught in school, of parents as marginal or even harmful in children's literacy development or of direct parental involvement in the teaching process as impracticable and undesirable. We have learned that much literacy — perhaps most — is learned at home, that parents or other family members are central to children's development, that parental exclusion is unjustifiable, and that involvement is feasible, rewarding, and can help meet the goals of schools and families.

References

ALBSU (1987) *Literacy, Numeracy and Adults: Evidence from the National Child Development Study*, London, Adult Literacy and Basic Skills Unit.

ALBSU (1993) *Parents and Their Children: The Intergenerational Effect of Poor Basic Skills*, London, Adult Literacy and Basic Skills Unit.

ALBSU (1994) *Family Literacy News, No. 2*, London, Adult Literacy and Basic Skills Unit.

ALLINGTON, R.L. (1980) 'Teacher interruption behavior during primary-grade oral reading', *Journal of Educational Psychology*, **1**, (3), pp.371–7.

ANBAR, A. (1986) 'Reading acquisition of pre-school children without systematic instruction', *Early Childhood Research Quarterly*, **1**, (1), pp.69–83.

APPLEBEE, A.N., LANGER, J.A. and MULLIS, I.V.S. (1988) *Who Reads Best? Factors Related to Reading Achievement in Grades 3, 7 and 11*, Princeton, NJ, Educational Testing Service.

ARNOLD, H. (1982) *Listening to Children Reading*, London, Hodder and Stoughton.

ASHTON, C., STONEY, A. and HANNON, P. (1986) 'A reading at home project in a first school', *Support for Learning*, **1**, (1), pp.43–49.

ATKIN, J., and BASTIANI, J. (1988) 'Training teachers to work with parents', in BASTIANI, J. (ed.) *Parents and Teachers 2: From Policy to Practice*, Windsor, NFER-Nelson.

BARTLETT, R., HALL, J. and NEALE, S. (1984) 'A parental involvement project in the primary schools of south Oxfordshire', *Reading*, **18**, (3), pp.173–7.

BASSEY, M. (1978) *Nine Hundred Primary School Teachers*, Windsor, NFER.

BECHER, R.M. (1985) 'Parent involvement and reading achievement: A review of research and implications for practice', *Childhood Education*, **62**, (September/October), pp.44–50.

BECKER, H.S. (1986) *Writing for Social Scientists*, Chicago, University of Chicago Press.

BELFIELD COMMUNITY SCHOOL (1974) *School Booklet*, unpublished document, Rochdale, Belfield Community School.

BENNETT, J. (1983) *Learning to Read with Picture Books*, Stroud, Thimble Press.

BEVERTON, S., HUNTER-CARSCH, M., OBRIST, C. and STUART, A. (1993) *Running Family*

Reading Groups: Guidelines on How to Develop Children's Voluntary Reading, Widnes, United Kingdom Reading Association.

BIRCHENOUGH, C. (1914) *History of Elementary Education in England and Wales*, London, University Tutorial Press.

BLOOM, W. (1987) *Partnership with Parents in Reading*, London, Hoddder and Stoughton.

BRIZIUS, J.A. and FOSTER, S.A. (1993) *Generation to Generation: Realizing the Promise of Family Literacy*, Ypsilanti, MI, High/Scope Press.

BRONFENBRENNER, U. (1974) *A Report on Longitudinal Evaluations of Preschool Programs, Vol. 2, Is Early Intervention Effective?* Washington, DC, DHEW. Publication No. (OHD), 74–25.

BROWN, C. (1975) *Literacy in 30 Hours: Paulo Freire's Process in North East Brazil*, London, Writers and Readers Publishing Cooperative.

BROWN, J.A.C. (1954) *The Social Psychology of Industry*, Harmondsworth, Penguin.

BRYANS, T., KIDD, A. and LEVEY, M. (1985) 'The Kings Heath Project', in TOPPING, K. and WOLFENDALE, S. (eds) *Parental Involvement in Children's Reading*, Beckenham, Croom Helm.

BRYANT, P. (1974) *Perception and Understanding in Young Children: An Experimental Approach*, London, Methuen.

BRYANT, P. and BRADLEY, L. (1985) *Children's Reading Problems*, Oxford, Basil Blackwell.

BURDETT, L. (1986) 'Two effective approaches for helping poor readers', *British Journal of Special Education*, **13**, (4), pp.151–4.

BUSHELL, R., MILLER, A. and ROBSON, D. (1982) 'Parents as remedial teachers: An account of a paired reading project with junior school failing readers and their parents', *Journal of the Association of Educational Psychologists*, **5**, (9), pp.7–13.

BYNNER, J. and FOGELMAN, K. (1993) 'Making the grade: Education and training experiences', in FERRI, E. (ed) *Life at 33: The Fifth Follow-up of the National Child Development Study*, London, National Children's Bureau.

CAMPBELL, D.T. and STANLEY, J.C. (1963) 'Experimental and quasi-experimental designs for research', in GAGE, N.L. (ed) *Handbook of Research on Teaching*, Chicago, Rand McNally.

CAMPBELL, R. (1981) 'An approach to analysing teacher verbal moves in hearing children read', *Journal of Research in Reading*, **4**, (1), pp.43–56.

CAMPBELL, R. (1988) *Hearing Children Read*, London, Routledge.

CATO, V. and WHETTON, C. (1991) *An Enquiry into Local Education Authority Evidence on Standards of Reading of Seven-year-old Children*, a report by the NFER, London, Department of Education and Science.

CENTRAL ADVISORY COUNCIL FOR EDUCATION (ENGLAND) (CACE) (1967) *Children and Their Primary Schools* (Plowden Report), London, HMSO.

CLARK, M. (1976) *Young Fluent Readers*, London, Heinemann Educational Books.

COLCOMBE, A. (1984) 'An analysis of the verbal interventions made by teachers and parents when helping some eight-year-old working class children read', unpublished MEd dissertation, University of Sheffield.

COMMISSION OF THE EUROPEAN COMMUNITIES (1988) *Report on the Fight Against Illiteracy. Social Europe, Supplement 2/88*, Luxembourg, Office for Official Publications of the European Communities.

CRAWFORD, A. (1983) 'Parental involvement and reading attainment: An investigation of a selection of the possible variables underlying the relationship, unpublished MEd dissertation (Educational Psychology), University of Exeter.

CYSTER, R., CLIFT, P.S. and BATTLE, S. (1980) *Parental Involvement in Primary Schools*, Windsor, NFER.

DARLING, S. and HAYES, A.E. (n.d.)*Breaking the Cycle of Illiteracy: The Kenan Family Literacy Model Program. Final Report, 1988–1989*, Louisville, KY, National Center for Family Literacy.

DAVID, A. (1983) 'Home-school links and reading', *Links*, **9**, (1), pp.8–10.

DAVIE, C.E., HUTT, S.J., VINCENT, E. and MASON, M. (1984) *The Young Child at Home*, Windsor, NFER-Nelson.

DAVIE, R., BUTLER, N. and GOLDSTEIN, H. (1972) *From Birth to Seven: A report of the National Child Development Study*, London, Longman/National Children's Bureau.

DEPARTMENT FOR EDUCATION (DFE) (1993) *English for Ages 5 to 16 (1993). Proposals of the Secretary of State for Education and the Secretary of State for Wales*, London, Department for Education.

DEPARTMENT OF EDUCATION AND SCIENCE (DES) (1975) *A Language for Life* (Bullock Report), London, HMSO.

DEPARTMENT OF EDUCATION AND SCIENCE (DES) (1978) *Primary Education in England: A Survey by HM Inspectors of Schools*, London, HMSO.

DEPARTMENT OF EDUCATION AND SCIENCE (DES) (1982) *Education 5 to 9: An Illustrative Survey of 80 First Schools in England*, London, HMSO.

DEPARTMENT OF EDUCATION AND SCIENCE (DES) (1989) *English in the National Curriculum*, London, HMSO.

DEPARTMENT OF EDUCATION AND SCIENCE (DES) (1990) *The Teaching and Learning of Reading in Primary Schools*, London, Department of Education and Science.

DOMBEY, H. and MEEK SPENCER, M. (eds) (1994) *First Steps Together: Home–School Early Literacy in European Contexts*, Oakhill, Trentham Books.

DONALDSON, M. (1978) *Children's Minds*, Glasgow, Fontana/Collins.

DOUGLAS, J.W.B. (1964) *The Home and the School: A study of Ability and Attainment in the Primary School*, London, MacGibbon and Kee.

DRUMMOND, A., GODFREY, L. and SATTIN, R. (1990) 'Promoting parental involvement in reading', *Support for Learning*, **5**, (3), pp.141–3.

DURKIN, D. (1966) *Children Who Read Early*, New York, Teachers College Press.

DYSON, J. and SWINSON, J. (1982) 'Involving parents in the teaching of reading: An account of a parent participation project involving failing readers in a primary school', *Journal of the Association of Educational Psychologist*, **5**, (9), pp.18–21.

EBBUTT, C.M. and BARBER, E. (1978) 'A homework reading scheme for backward readers in a secondary school', *Reading*, **13**, (2), pp.25–31.

Edwards, A.D. (1976) *Language in Culture and Class: The Sociology of Language and Education*, London, Heinemann Educational Books.

EDWARDS, P.A. (1989) 'Supporting lower SES mothers' attempts to provide scaffolding for book reading', in J. ALLEN and MASON, J.M. (eds) *Risk Makers, Risk Takers, Risk Breakers: Reducing the Risks for Young Literacy Learners*, Portsmouth, NH, Heinemann.

EISENSTEIN, E.L. (1985) 'On the printing press as an agent of change', in OLSON, D.R., TORRANCE, N. and HILDYARD, A. (eds) *Literacy, Language and Learning: The Nature and Consequences of Reading and Writing*, Cambridge, Cambridge University Press.

EKINSMYTH, C. and BYNNER, J. (1994) *The Basic Skills of Young Adults: Some Findings from the 1970 British Cohort Study*, London, Adult Literacy and Basic Skills Unit.

ENGLEMANN, S., HADDOX, P. and BRUNER, E. (1983) *Teach Your Child to Read in 100 Easy Lessons*, New York, Simon and Schuster.

FARQUHAR, C., BLATCHFORD, P., BURKE, J., PLEWIS, I. and TIZARD, B. (1985) 'A comparison of the views of parents and reception teachers', *Education pp. 3–13*, **13**, pp.17–22.

FOGELMAN, K. and GOLDSTEIN, H. (1976) 'Social factors associated with changes in educational attainment', *Educational Studies*, **2**, pp.95–109.

FRANCIS, H. (1987) 'Hearing beginning readers: Problems of relating practice to theory in interpretation and evaluation', *British Educational Research Journal*, **13**, (3), pp.215–25.

FREIRE, P. (1970) *Pedagogy of the Oppressed*, New York, Herder and Herder.

FREIRE, P. (1972) *Cultural Action for Freedom*, Harmondsworth, Penguin.

FRENCH, H.J. (1989) 'Listening to children read: An analysis of teachers' responses', unpublished MEd dissertation, University of Sheffield.

FRIEND, P. (1983) Reading and the parent: After the Haringey Project, *Reading*, **17**, (1), pp.7–12.

GLYNN, T. and McNAUGHTON, S. (1985) 'The Mangere Home and School remedial reading procedures: Continuing research on their effectiveness', *New Zealand Journal of Psychology*, **14**, pp.66–77.

GOELMAN, H., OBERG, A.A. and SMITH, F. (eds) (1984) *Awakening to Literacy*, Portsmouth, NH, Heinemann.

GOLDSMITH, E. and HANDEL, R. (1990) *Family Reading: An Intergenerational Approach to Literacy*, Syracuse, NY, New Readers Press.

GOODMAN, K. (1969) 'Analysis of oral reading miscues: Applied psycholinguistics', *Reading Research Quarterly*, **5**, (1), pp.9–30.

GOODMAN, K. (1986) *What's Whole in Whole Language?* Portsmouth, NH, Heinemann Educational Books.

GOODMAN, Y.M. (1980) 'The roots of literacy', in M.P. DOUGLAS, (ed) *Claremont Reading Conference Forty-fourth Yearbook*, Claremont, CA, Claremont Reading Conference.

GOODMAN, Y.M. (1986) 'Children coming to know literacy', in TEALE, W.H. and SULZBY, E. (eds) *Emergent Literacy: Writing and Reading*, Norwood, NJ, Ablex Publishing Corporation.

GOSWAMI, U. and BRYANT, P. (1990) *Phonological Skills and Learning to Read*, Hove, Lawrence Erlbaum Associates.

GRAFF, H. (1991) '*The Literacy Myth: Cultural Integration and Social Structure in the Nineteenth Century*, 2nd edn, New Brunswick, NJ, Transaction Publishers.

GRAY, J. (1979) 'Reading progress in English infant schools: Some problems emerging from a study of teacher effectiveness', *British Educational Research Journal*, **5**, (2), pp.141–57.

GREEN, C. (1987) 'Parental facilitation of young children's writing', *Early Child Development and Care*, **28**, pp.31–37.

GREENING, M. and SPENCELY, J. (1987) 'Shared reading: Support for inexperienced readers', *Educational Psychology in Practice*, April, pp.31–37.

GRIFFITHS, A. and EDMONDS, M. (1986) *Report on the Calderdale Pre-school Parent Book Project*, Halifax, England, School's Psychological Service, Calderdale Education Department.

GRIFFITHS, A. and HAMILTON, D. (1984) *Parent, Teacher, Child: Working Together in Children's Learning*, London, Methuen.

GRIFFITHS, A. and KING, A. (1985) 'PACT: Development of home-reading schemes in ILEA', in TOPPING, K. and WOLFENDALE, S. (eds) *Parental Involvement in Children's Reading*, Beckenham, Croom Helm.

GULLIVER, J. (1979) 'Teachers' assumptions in listening to reading', *Language for Learning*, **1**, (1), pp.42–56.

HALL, N. (1987) *The Emergence of Literacy*, London, Hodder and Stoughton.

HALL, N., HERRING, G., HENN, H. and CRAWFORD, L. (1989) *Parental Views on Writing and the Teaching of Writing*, Manchester, Manchester Polytechnic School of Education.

HANDEL, R. (1992) 'The partnership for Family Reading: Benefits for families and schools, *The Reading Teacher*, **46**, (2), pp.116–25.

HANDEL, R. and GOLDSMITH, E. (1988) 'Intergenerational literacy: The Parent Readers Program', paper presented to the Annual Meeting of the American Educational Research Association, New Orleans, LA.

HANNON, P. (1986) 'Teachers' and parents' experiences of parental involvement in the teaching of reading', *Cambridge Journal of Education*, **16**, (1), pp.28–37.

HANNON, P. (1987) 'A study of the effects of parental involvement in the teaching of reading on children's reading test performance', *British Journal of Educational Psychology*, **57**, pp.56–72.

HANNON, P. (1989) 'How should parental involvement in the teaching of reading be evaluated?' *British Educational Research Journal*, **15**, (1), pp.33–40.

HANNON, P. (1990) 'Parental involvement in preschool literacy development', in WRAY, D. (ed) *Emerging Partnerships: Current Research in Language and*

Literacy, BERA Dialogues in Education, 4, Clevedon, Avon, Multilingual Matters.

HANNON, P. (1993) 'Conditions of learning at home and in school', in MERTTENS, R., MAYERS, D., BROWN, A. and VASS, J. (eds) *Ruling the Margins: Problematising Parental Involvement*, London, University of North London Press.

HANNON, P. and CUCKLE, P. (1984) 'Parental involvement in the teaching of reading: A study of current school practice', *Educational Research*, **26**, (1), pp.7–13.

HANNON, P. and JACKSON, A. (1987a) 'Educational home visiting and the teaching of reading', *Educational Research*, **29**, (3) pp.182–91.

HANNON, P. and JACKSON, A. (1987b) *The Belfield Reading Project Final Report*, London, National Children's Bureau.

HANNON, P. and JAMES, S. (1990) 'Parents' and teachers' perspectives on preschool literacy development', *British Educational Research Journal*, **16**, (3), pp.259–72.

HANNON, P. and McNALLY, J. (1986) 'Children's understanding and cultural factors in reading test performance', *Educational Review*, **38**, (3), pp.269–80.

HANNON, P. and WELCH, J. (1993) 'Bringing parents into initial teacher education in the context of a school partnership', *Educational Review*, **45**, (3), pp.279–91.

HANNON, P., JACKSON, A. and PAGE, B. (1985) 'Implementation and take-up of a project to involve parents in the teaching of reading', in TOPPING, K. and WOLFENDALE, S. (eds) *Parental Involvement in Children's Reading*, London, Croom Helm.

HANNON, P., JACKSON, A. and WEINBERGER, J. (1986a) 'Parents and teachers strategies in hearing young children read', *Research Papers in Education*, **1**, (1), pp.6–25.

HANNON, P., WEINBERGER, J. and NUTBROWN, C. (1991) 'A study of work with parents to promote early literacy development', *Research Papers in Education*, **6**, (2), pp.77–97.

HANNON, P., WEINBERGER, J., PAGE, B. and JACKSON, A. (1986b) 'Home–school communication by means of reading cards', *British Educational Research Journal*, **12**, (3), pp.269–80.

HARSTE, J.C., WOODWARD, V.A. and BURKE, C.L. (1984) *Language stories and literacy lessons*, Portsmouth, NH, Heinemann Educational Books.

HEATH, A. (1981) 'A paired reading programme', *Edition 2* (ILEA Schools' Psychological Service), **2**, pp.22–32.

HEATH, S.B. (1982) 'What no bedtime story means: Narrative skills at home and school', *Language in Society*, **11**, pp.49–76.

HEATH, S.B. (1983) *Ways with Words: Language, Life and Work in Communities and Classrooms*, Cambridge, Cambridge University Press.

HER MAJESTY'S INSPECTORATE (HMI) (1989) *The Education of Children Under Five*, London, HMSO.

HERSEN, M. and BARLOW, D.M. (1977) *Single-case Experiment Designs: Strategies for Studying Behavior Change*, New York, Pergamon.

Hewison, J. (1988) 'The long term effectiveness of parental involvement in reading: A follow-up to the Haringey Reading Project', *British Journal of Educational Psychology*, **58**, pp.184–90.

Hewison, J. and Tizard, J. (1980) 'Parental involvement and reading attainment', *British Journal of Educational Psychology*, **50**, pp.209–15.

Hirst, K. and Hannon, P. (1990) 'An evaluation of a preschool home teaching project', *Educational Research*, **32**, (1), pp.33–39.

Hoffman, J.V. and Baker, C. (1981) 'Characterizing teacher feedback to student miscues during oral reading instruction', *The Reading Teacher*, **34**, (8), pp.907–13.

Hoffman, J.V. and Kugle, C.L. (1982) 'A study of theoretical orientation to reading and its relationship to teacher verbal feedback during reading instruction', *Journal of Classroom Interaction*, **18**, (1), pp.2–7.

Hoffman, J.V., O'Neal, S., Kastler, L., Clements, R., Segel, K. and Nash, M. (1984) 'Guided oral reading and miscue focused verbal feedback in second-grade classrooms', *Reading Research Quarterly*, **19**, (3), pp.367–84.

Hoffman, S. (1982) 'Parent's teaching strategies with children learning to read and write: Before and after classroom instruction', paper presented at the Annual Convention of the International Reading Association, Chicago, April.

Hunter-Grundin, E. and Grundin, H.U. (1980) *Hunter-Grundin Literacy Profiles. Reference Books for Level One and Level Two*, High Wycombe, The Test Agency.

Jackson, A. and Hannon, P. (1981) *The Belfield Reading Project*, Rochdale, Belfield Community Council.

Johnston, P. (1984) 'Prior knowledge and reading comprehension test bias', *Reading Research Quarterly*, **19**, pp.219–39.

Johnston, P.H. (1985) 'Understanding reading disability: A case study approach', *Harvard Educational Review*, **55**, (2), pp.153–77.

Jowett, S. and Baginsky, M. (1988) 'Parents and education: A survey of their involvement and a discussion of some issues', *Educational Research*, **30**, (1), pp.36–45.

Kemp, M. (1992) 'There's more to listening than meets the ear: Interactions between oral readers and their parents as tutors', *International Journal of Disability, Development and Education*, **39**, (3), pp.197–223.

Kirsch, I.S., Jungeblut, A., Jenkins, L. and Kolstad, A. (1993) *Executive Summary from 'Adult Literacy in America': A First Look at the Results of the National Adult Literacy Survey*, September, Princeton, NJ, Educational Testing Service.

Kohl, H. (1974) *Reading, How to*, Harmondsworth, Penguin.

Lankshear, C. (1987) *Literacy, Schooling and Revolution*, London, Falmer Press.

Lareau, A. (1989) *Home Advantage: Social Class and Parental Involvement in Elementary Education*, London, Falmer Press.

Lazar, I., Darlington, R., Murray, H., Royce, J. and Snipper, A. (1982) 'Lasting effects of early education', *Monographs of the Society for Research in Child Development*, **47**, (2–3, Serial No. 195).

LEACH, D.J. and SIDDALL, S.W. (1990) 'Parental involvement in the teaching of reading: A comparison of hearing reading, paired reading, pause, prompt and praise, and direct instruction methods', *British Journal of Educational Psychology*, **60**, pp.349–55.

LELER, H. (1983) 'Parent education and involvement in relation to the schools and to parents of school-aged children', in R. HASKINS and D. ADAMS (eds) *Parent Education and Public Policy*, Norwood, NJ, Ablex Publishing Corporation.

LINDSAY, G., EVANS, A. and JONES, B. (1985) 'Paired reading versus relaxed reading: A comparison', *British Journal of Educational Psychology*, **55**, pp.304–9.

LOCKE, J.L. (1988) 'Pittsburgh's beginning with books project', *School Library Journal*, February, pp.22–24.

LONG, R. (1986) *Developing Parental Involvement: A Practical Guide for Nursery, First, and Primary Schools*, London, Macmillan.

LUJAN, M.E., STOLWORTHY, D.L. and WOODEN, S.L. (1986) *A Parent Training Early Intervention Programme in Preschool Literacy*, ERIC (Educational Resources Information Centre) Descriptive Report, ED 270 988.

LUKE, A. (1988) *Literacy, Textbooks and Ideology*, London, Falmer Press.

McCORMICK, C.E., and MASON, J.M. (1986) 'Intervention procedures for increasing preschool children's interest in and knowledge about reading', in TEALE, W. and SULZBY, E. (eds) *Emergent Literacy: Writing and Reading*, Norwood, NJ, Ablex Publishing Corporation.

McIVOR, M.C. (1990) *Family Literacy in Action: A Survey of Successful Programs*, Syracuse, NY, New Readers Press.

MACLEAN, M., BRYANT, P. and BRADLEY, L. (1987) 'Rhymes, nursery rhymes, and reading in early childhood', *Merrill-Palmer Quarterly*, **33**, (3), pp.255–81.

McNAUGHTON, S. and GLYNN, T. (1981) 'Delayed versus immediate attention to oral reading errors: Effects on accuracy and self-correction', *Educational Psychology*, **1**, (1), pp.57–65.

McNAUGHTON, S.S., GLYNN, T. and ROBINSON, V. (1981) *Parents as Remedial Tutors: Issues for Home and School*, Wellington, New Zealand Council for Educational Research.

MEEK, M. (1982) *Learning to Read*, London, The Bodley Head.

MILLER, A. (1987) 'Is there still a place for paired reading?' *Educational Psychology in Practice*, April, 38–43.

MILLER, A., ROBSON, D. and BUSHELL, R. (1986) 'Parental participation in paired reading: A controlled study', *Educational Psychology*, **6**, (3), pp.277–84.

MITCHELL, K.A. (1980) 'Patterns of teacher–student responses to oral reading errors as related to teachers' theoretical frameworks', *Research in the Teaching of English*, **14**, (3), pp.243–63.

MORGAN, R. (1976) 'Paired reading tuition: A preliminary report on a technique for cases of reading deficit', *Child Care Health and Development*, **2**, pp.13–28.

MORGAN, R. and LYON, E. (1979) 'Paired reading: A preliminary report on a technique for parental tuition of reading-retarded children', *Journal of Child Psychology and Psychiatry*, **20**, pp.151–60.

References

NATIONAL FOUNDATION FOR EDUCATIONAL RESEARCH (NFER) (1973) *Manual of Instructions for Reading Test A*, Windsor, NFER.

NEALE, M. (1966) *Neale Analysis of Reading Ability*, Basingstoke, Macmillan Education, (2nd edn.)

NEWSON, J. and NEWSON, E. (1977) *Perspectives on School at Seven Years Old*, London, Allen and Unwin.

NICKSE, R.S. (1990) *Family and Intergenerational Literacy Programs: An Update of 'Noises of Literacy'*, Columbus, OH, ERIC Clearinghouse on Adult, Career and Vocational Education, Ohio State University.

NICKSE, R.S. (1993) 'A typology of family and intergenerational literacy programmes: Implications for evaluation', *Viewpoints*, **15**, pp.34–40.

NURSS, J. (1993) 'Family Literacy programs: Effects on young children', paper presented to the Annual Meeting of the American Educational Research Association, Atlanta, GA, April.

NURSS, J., HUSS, R. and HANNON, P. (1993) American parents hearing children read: Trying a British approach, *International Journal of Early Childhood*, **25**, (2), pp.20–26.

NUTBROWN, C. and HANNON, P. (1993) 'Assessing early literacy: New measures needed', *International Journal of Early Childhood*, **25**, (2), pp.27–30.

NUTBROWN, C., HANNON, P. and WEINBERGER, J. (1991) 'Training teachers to work with parents to promote early literacy development', *International Journal of Early Childhood*, **23**, (2), pp.1–10.

OBRIST, C. (1978) *How to Run Family Reading Groups*, Ormskirk, United Kingdom Reading Association.

PEARCE, L. (1992) 'Partners in literacy: Organising Parents as Tutors programmes in Cambridgeshire primary schools', *Links*, **17**, (1), pp.10–12.

POSTMAN, N. (1970) 'The politics of reading', *Harvard Educational Review*, **40**, (2), pp.244–52.

PRITCHARD, D. and RENNIE, J. (1978) *Reading: Involving Parents*, Coventry, Coventry Education Committee, Community Education Project.

PUMFREY, P. (1985) *Reading: Tests and Assessment Techniques*, 2nd edn, Sevenoaks, Hodder and Stoughton.

PUMFREY, P. (1986) 'Paired reading: Promise and pitfalls', *Educational Research*, **28**, (2), pp.89–94.

PUMFREY, P., and LEE, J. (1982) 'Cultural group, reading attainments and dialect interference', *Journal of Research in Reading*, **5**, pp.133–46.

RADICAL STATISTICS EDUCATION GROUP (1982) *Reading Between the Numbers: A Critical Guide to Educational Research*, London, BSSRS Publications.

RAIM, J. (1980) 'Who learns when parents teach children?' *The Reading Teacher*, **33**, pp.152–5.

RASINSKI, T.V. (1989) 'Reading and the empowerment of parents', *The Reading Teacher*, **43**, (3), pp.226–31.

RENNIE, J. (ed) (1985) *British Community Primary Schools*, London, Falmer Press.

REYNOLDS, R.E., TAYLOR, M.A., STEFFENSEN, M.S., SHIREY, L.L. and ANDERSON, R.C.

(1982) 'Cultural schemata and reading comprehension', *Reading Research Quarterly*, **17**, pp.353–66.

ROSE, T.L., MCENTIRE, E. and DOWDY, C. (1982) 'Effects of two error-correction procedures on oral reading', *Learning Disability Quarterly*, **5**, (2), pp.100–105.

RYBACK, D. and STAATS, W. (1970) 'Parents as behaviour therapy-technicians in treating reading deficits (dyslexia)', *Journal of Behaviour Therapy and Experimental Psychiatry*, **1**, pp.109–19.

SEAMAN, D., POPP, B. and DARLING, S. (1991) *Follow-up Study of the Impact of the Kenan Trust model for Family Literacy*, Louisville, KY, National Center for Family Literacy.

SEGEL, E. and FRIEDBERG, J.B. (1991) ' "Is today Liberry Day?" Community support for family literacy', *Language Arts*, **68**, December, pp.654–7.

SIMON, B. (1960) *Studies in the History of Education, 1780–1870*, London, Lawrence and Wishart.

SIMON, B. (ed) (1972) *The Radical Tradition in Education in Britain*, London, Lawrence and Wishart.

SMITH, F. (1973) *Psycholinguistics and Reading*, New York, Holt, Rinehart and Winston.

SMITH, F. (1988) *Joining the Literacy Club*, Portsmouth, NH, Heinemann.

SMITH, G. (ed) (1975) *Educational Priority. Vol. 4 The West Riding Project*, London, HMSO.

SNOW, C. (1991) 'The theoretical basis for relationships between language and literacy in development', *Journal of Research in Childhood Education*, **6**, (1), pp.5–10.

SOUTHGATE, V. (1959) *Southgate Group Reading Tests*, London; Hodder and Stoughton.

SPALDING, B., DREW, R., ELLBECK, J., LIVESEY, J., MUSSET, M. and WALES, D. (1984) ' "If you want to improve your reading ask your mum" — An attempt to involve parents in the reading process at secondary age level', *Remedial Education*, **19**, (4), pp.157–61.

SPIEGEL, D.L. and ROGERS, C. (1980) 'Teacher responses to miscues during oral reading by second-grade students', *Journal of Educational Research*, **74**, (1), pp.8–12.

STAFFORD, L.S. and BAYER, C.L. (1993) *Interaction Between Parents and Children*, Newbury Park, CA, Sage.

STEFFENSEN, M.S., JOAG-DEV, C. and ANDERSON, R.C. (1979) 'A cross-cultural perspective on reading comprehension', *Reading Research Quarterly*, **15**, pp.1–15.

STIERER, B. (1985) 'School reading volunteers: Results of a postal survey of primary school head teachers in England', *Journal of Research in Reading*, **8**, (1), pp.21–31.

ST. PIERRE, R., SWARTZ, J., MURRAY, S., LANGHORST, B. and NICKEL, P. (1993) *National Evaluation of the Even Start Family Literacy Program. Second Interim*

Report, Washington, DC, US Department of Education, Office of Policy and Planning.

STREET, B. (1984) *Literacy in Theory and Practice,* Cambridge, Cambridge University Press.

SWINSON, J. (1985) 'A parental involvement project in a nursery school', *Educational Psychology in Practice,* **1**, (1), pp.19–22.

SWINSON, J.M. (1986) 'Paired reading: A critique', *Support for Learning,* **1**, (2), pp.29–32.

TAYLOR, D. (1983) *Family Literacy: Young Children Learning to Read and Write,* Exeter, NH, Heinemann.

TAYLOR, D. and DORSEY-GAINES, C. (1988) *Growing up Literate: Learning from Inner-city Families,* Portsmouth, NH, Heinemann.

TAYLOR, P.H., EXON, G. and HOLLEY, B. (1972) *A Study of Nursery Education, Schools Council Working Paper 41,* London, Evans/Methuen Educational.

TEALE, W.H. (1986) 'Home background and young children's literacy development', in TEALE, W.H. and SULZBY, E. (eds) *Emergent Literacy: Writing and Reading,* Norwood, NJ, Ablex Publishing Corporation.

TEALE, W.H. and SULZBY, E. (eds) (1986) *Emergent Literacy: Writing and Reading,* Norwood, NJ, Ablex Publishing Corporation.

TIZARD, B. (1977) 'Play: The child's way of learning?' in TIZARD, B. and HARVEY, D. (eds) *Biology of Play,* London, Heinemann Medical.

TIZARD, B. and HUGHES, M. (1984) *Young Children Learning: Talking and Thinking at Home and in School,* London, Fontana.

TIZARD, J., MOSS, P. and PERRY, J. (1976) *All Our Children: Pre-school Services in a Changing Society,* London, Temple Smith.

TIZARD, J., SCHOFIELD, W.N. and HEWISON, J. (1982) 'Collaboration between teachers and parents in assisting children's reading', *British Journal of Educational Psychology,* **52**, pp.1–15.

TIZARD, B., BLATCHFORD, P., BURKE, J., FARQUHAR, C. and PLEWIS, I. (1988) *Young Children at School in the Inner City,* London, Lawrence Erlbaum Associates.

TOEPRITZ, P.I. (1982) 'A study of parent–child interaction in a paired reading project', Unpublished MSc (Educational Psychology) Special Study, University of Sheffield.

TOOMEY, D. (1993) 'Parents hearing their children read: A review. Rethinking the lessons of the Haringey Project', *Educational Research,* **35**, (3), pp.223–36.

TOPPING, K. (1985) 'Review and prospect', in TOPPING, K. and WOLFENDALE, S. (eds) *Parental Involvement in Children's Reading,* London, Croom Helm.

TOPPING, K. (1986) 'WHICH parental involvement in reading scheme? A guide for practitioners', *Reading,* **20**, (3), pp.148–56.

TOPPING, K.J. and LINDSAY, G. (1991) 'The structure and development of the paired reading technique', *Journal of Research in Reading,* **15**, (2), pp.120–36.

TOPPING, K.J. and LINDSAY, G. (1992) 'Paired reading: A review of the literature', *Research Papers in Education,* **7**, (3), pp.199–246.

Topping, K. and Wolfendale, S. (eds) (1985) *Parental Involvement in Children's Reading*, London, Croom Helm.

UNESCO (1988) *1990: International Literacy Year (ILY)*, ED/ILY/88.10, Paris, UNESCO.

Vincent, D., Green, L., Francis, J. and Powney, J. (1983) *A Review of Reading Tests*, Windsor, NFER-Nelson.

Vinograd-Bausell, C.R. and Bausell, R.B. (1987) 'Home teaching of word recognition skills', *Journal of Research and Development in Education*, **20**, (3), pp.57–64.

Vygotsky, L.S. (1962) *Thought and Language*, Cambridge, MA, MIT Press.

Wade, B. (1984) *Story at Home and School. Educational Review Publication Number 10*, Birmingham, University of Birmingham, Faculty of Education.

Wade, B. and Moore, M. (1993) *Bookstart in Birmingham, Book Trust Report No.2*, London, Book Trust.

Walker, C. (1975) *Teaching Prereading Skills*, London, Ward Lock Educational.

Wareing, L. (1985) 'A comparative study of three methods of parental involvement in the teaching of reading', in Topping, K. and Wolfendale, S. (eds) *Parental Involvement in Children's Reading*, London, Croom Helm.

Waterland, L. (1985) *Read with Me: An Apprenticeship Approach to Reading*, Stroud, Thimble Press.

Webb, M., Webb, T. and Eccles, G. (1985) 'Parental participation in the teaching of reading', *Remedial Education*, **20**, (2), pp.86–91.

Wedge, P. and Prosser, H. (1973) *Born to Fail?* London, Arrow Books/National Children's Bureau.

Weikart, D.P., Epstein, A.S., Shweinhart, L.J. and Bond, J.T. (1978) *The Ypsilanti Preschool Curriculum Demonstration Project: Preschool Years and Longitudinal Results (Monographs of the High/Scope Educational Research Foundation, 4)*, Ypsilanti, MI, High/Scope Press.

Weinberg, P. (1990) *Family Literacy and the School*, Syracuse, NY, New Readers Press.

Weinberger, J. (1983) *The Fox Hill Reading Workshop*, London, Family Service Units.

Weinberger, J., Hannon, P. and Nutbrown, C. (1990) *Ways of Working with Parents to Promote Early Literacy Development, USDE Papers in Education, No.14*, Sheffield, University of Sheffield Division of Education.

Weinberger, J., Jackson, A. and Hannon, P. (1986) 'Variation in take-up of a project to involve parents in the teaching of reading', *Educational Studies*, **12**, (2), pp.159–74.

Wells, G. (1978) 'Language use and educational success: An empirical response to Joan Tough's "The Development of Meaning" (1977)', *Research in Education*, **18**, pp.9–34.

Wells, G. (1985) *Language Development in the Pre-school Years*, Cambridge, Cambridge University Press.

Wells, G. (1987) *The Meaning Makers: Children Learning Language and Using Language to Learn*, London, Hodder and Stoughton.

WHITBREAD, N. (1972) *The Evolution of the Nursery-Infant School: A History of Infant and Nursery Education in Britain, 1800–1970*, London, Routledge and Kegan Paul.

WHITE, P., SOLITY, J. and REEVE, C. (1984) 'Teaching parents to teach reading', *Special Education: Forward Trends*, **11**, (1), pp.11–13.

WHITEHURST, E.A. (1983) 'A Survey of Parental Involvement in the Early Reading Attainment of Middle Class Children', unpublished MEd dissertation, Division of Education, University of Sheffield.

WIDLAKE, P. and MACLEOD, F. (1984) *Raising Standards: Parental Involvement Programmes and the Language Performance of Children*, Coventry, Community Education Development Centre.

WILBY, P. (1981) 'The Belfield Experiment', *Sunday Times*, 29 March.

WINTER, M. and ROUSE, J. (1990) 'Fostering intergenerational literacy: The Missouri Parents as Teachers programme', *The Reading Teaching*, **24**, (2), pp.382–6.

WINTER, S. (1990) 'Paired reading: Two questions', *Educational Psychology in Practice*, **6**, (2), pp.96–99.

WOODHEAD, M. (ed) (1976) *An Experiment in Nursery Education*, Windsor, NFER.

YOUNG, D. (1980) *Manual for the Group Reading Test*, Sevenoaks, Hodder and Stoughton, (2nd edn).

YOUNG, P. and TYRE, C. (1983) *Dyslexia or Illiteracy?* Milton Keynes, Open University Press.

Author Index

ALBSU (Adult Literacy and Basic Skills Unit) 4, 7, 8, 105, 107
Allington, R.L. 89
Anbar, A. 60
Applebee, A.N. 47, 148
Arnold, H. 86, 87, 88, 98
Ashton, C. 82, 119, 139, 141
Atkin, J. 20, 49

Baginsky, M. 27, 31
Baker, C. 89
Barlow, D.M. 126
Barber, E. 148
Bartlett, R. 141
Bassey, M. 86
Bastiani, J. 20, 149
Battle, S. 27
Bausell, R.B. 102, 144
Bayer, C.L. 104
Becher, R.M. 144
Becker, H.S. 3
Belfield Community School 22
Bell, A. 14
Bennett, J. 73
Beverton, S. 25, 103, 148
Birchenough, C. 15
Bloom, W. 140
Bradley, L. 72
Brizius, J.A. 105, 106
Bronfenbrenner, U. 63
Brown, C. 10
Brown, J.A.C. 125
Bryans, T. 25, 101, 142
Bryant, P. 72, 117
Burdett, L. 141, 143
Bushell, R. 24, 99, 119
Bynner, J. 8, 107, 108

CACE (Central Advisory Council for Education) 20, 26, 30, 47, 87

Campbell, D.T. 120, 124
Campbell, R. 90, 91, 98
Carmichael, H. 37
Cato, V. 6
Clark, M. 60
Clift, P.S. 27
Colcombe, A. 91
Commission of the European Communities 9
Crawford, A. 141
Cuckle, P. 22, 28, 88
Cyster, R. 27, 75

Darling, S. 146
David, A. 141
Davie, C.E. 37
Davie, R. 9, 42, 43
DES (Department of Education and Science) 6, 15, 19, 26, 29, 30, 31, 45, 49, 58, 86, 87
DFE (Department for Education) 50
Dombey, H. 57
Donaldson, M. 7, 117
Dorsey-Gaines, C. 41, 60, 104
Douglas, J.W.B. 43
Drummond, A. 143
Durkin, D. 60
Dyson, J. 141

Ebbutt, C.M. 148
Edmonds, M. 65, 67, 145
Edwards, A.D. 44, 117
Edwards, P.A. 66, 67, 107
Eisenstein, E.L. 3
Ekinsmyth, C. 8
Englemann, S. 102

Farquhar, C. 29, 45, 52
Fogelman, K. 9, 107, 108
Foster, S.A. 105, 106

Subject Index